A BOOK FOR MINDFUL ENTREPRENEURS.

BORN TO BE *an* ENTREPRENEUR

KRISTYNA ZAPLETAL

Contents

BORN TO BE *an* ENTREPRENEUR

BIRD & SOUL
PRESS

Entrepreneurship

1. Kill That Beautiful Beast

Maybe you've once considered running your own business. Maybe you wish to assume control of your time and money. Maybe you dream of being your own boss. And maybe you wish to leave a footprint on this world.

Whichever the case, some of the following may have—possibly more than once—crossed your mind.

> I don't have enough experience. I don't have enough time. I lack confidence. My background is far from privileged. My starting point was pretty low. I lack the necessary skills. I'm too old. I'm too young. I'm short of money. I'm not ready to leave my current job.

...which might have brought you to a conclusion that you were simply not meant to be an ENTREPRENEUR.

And perhaps you were right.

The idea of becoming a person who creates their own rules, who has control over their life, and who makes a positive impact on people around them has remained attractive, yet too abstract and distant to attain for you.

You'd rather wait for the perfect conditions.

The day when you accumulate sufficient capital. The day when you meet the ideal partner. The day when you strike just the right idea. The day when you are strong enough to build a project from scratch and lead others.

Yet, deep inside you know this PERFECT DAY IS MERELY A FANTASY.

It doesn't exist and it will never arrive. It is a fabulous creature that has nested in your mind, feeding on your doubts and on the inhibiting fear of failure.

If you make a deliberate choice to keep it alive and marvel at its beauty, it will gradually poison you with regrets and dejection.

The moment you resolve to kill it, the spirit of entrepreneurship will instantly start filling its place.

YOU'RE NOT A VICTIM OF EXTERNAL CIRCUMSTANCES, YOU'RE A VICTIM OF YOUR INABILITY TO DEAL WITH THEM.

2. Dogs Can Always Tell

You are who you believe you are.

Such an affirmation may sound simplistic or even banal, but it is correct and it is something you must hold on to.

Only you yourself choose how the rest of the world sees you. And no one can tell you otherwise unless your body gives away signals that contradict what you say out loud. Our mind is a powerful instrument and it can fundamentally transform how we act on the outside, yet only if we have control over our thoughts.

Take what happens when someone treats you wrong, for instance. Negative thoughts start racing, and as a result awful emotions accumulate to make you feel miserable. Although in theory you can eliminate them both, thus preventing them from poisoning your beliefs and behavior, it's not an easy feat. Before you even know it, you indulge in the dramatic spectacle that steals the main stage. The more you clap, the more absorbing the gruesome show gets, depleting your energy reserves and causing cracks in your self-image.

It's not the world that keeps fighting you no matter how hard you try. Your only true enemy resides right there, in your head. YOU'RE NOT A VICTIM OF EXTERNAL CIRCUMSTANCES, YOU'RE A VICTIM OF YOUR INABILITY TO DEAL WITH THEM.

If your mind suspects you're not good enough to do something, it has likely already assisted you in making it a reality. So if you think you're not ready to be an entrepreneur, then you're not ready. But don't blame your poor education, inadequate experience, or scarce funds.

On the contrary, if you value your potential in earnest, it will reflect in your gestures, facial expressions, movements, your posture, and in any word that leaves your mouth.

Imagine for a moment what your life would look like if you achieved something big. Let's fantasize.

You would improve lives of many. People would respect and admire you. As a consequence, it would be relatively easy to make money and achieve material comfort. Your family would be pleased and proud.

Close your eyes and dream.

Where would you live? How would you dress? What car would you drive? What type of people would you meet?

Can you see it? Can you see how you walk? How your posture has changed? How your voice has gotten stronger and your manners more self-assured? And how others treat you differently?

I exude confidence.

=

I appreciate and I trust in my qualities and abilities.

Success generates more success. When someone assumes they deserve to succeed, it happens again and again to them. They seem to achieve anything they want. Besides, people around them contagiously adopt the same conviction.

Humans resemble dogs in one thing. If you're scared, it's hard to fool a dog to believe otherwise. They simply pick up on the physiological changes you experience as a response to a stress situation. The same goes for hiding cracks in your self-esteem when dealing with fellow humans. Much as you can train yourself to act with utmost poise and boldness, people will sniff out your deficient sense of worthiness, which does reflect in your body language whether you want it to or not.

Learn to understand and respect your value.

In no way does it mean to become delusional. It means to discover what your place on Earth is and uncover your purpose.

A tricky task but not impossible.

3. Looking Into the Mirror

So is there something we can do if we lack either the time, resources, experience, or skills to embrace the road of entrepreneurship?

The answer is: START WALKING.

You really need only one thing right now and that is will-power. As you are about to learn eventually, you can make time work for, not against, you. A replete bank account certainly helps when launching a business, but it's not a prerequisite for addressing people's needs or solving their problems. And experience and skill don't occur by themselves, they need to be cultivated.

If you look into a mirror, what do you see? Do you see an entrepreneur? Do you trust your own reflection? Is there a force driving your forward, despite the dictate of the conventional wisdom?

If you say yes, then it doesn't matter where you live. It doesn't matter if you are twenty or sixty-five. It's not important if you have a flair for art or talent for mathematics.

You're able to create value, both for yourself and for others. You can make a difference. And you can do it as of today.

Entrepreneurs undertake challenging and risky tasks. They move mountains. They accomplish things others can barely grasp. And they couldn't do so without courage, constant self-improvement, and hard work. However, , to shield themselves with a perfect resume, or to hinge on strikes of luck.

If you aspire to be an entrepreneur, master your own thoughts in the first place. Having control over your mind makes it possible for you to control your whole life, and as a result to shape the world around you.

Also, in order to offer authentic value to others, you need to learn to become completely honest with yourself. Only then can you make sure you're on the right way. If you can't trust yourself, you will inevitably end up betraying others. And they will be able to tell in a flash.

THERE IS NO PERFECT DAY. THERE IS NO PERFECT SITUATION. THERE IS NO PERFECT PERSON. IT'S ONLY YOU. ONLY YOU DECIDE WHO YOU ARE. ONLY YOU DECIDE WHERE YOU GO.

4. Looking Around and Beyond

*Y*our social reality is made up of five interconnected layers.

First, it's **YOU**. You are composed of your body (organs, systems, senses), your soul (consciousness, reason, emotions, will), and your spirit (intuition, faith, conscience, hope, love).

Then there's your **INNER CIRCLE**. These are the closest people in your life, your family, your good friends, your life partner.

Our relationships with these individuals are usually driven by strong emotions, such as affection, attachment, dependence, respect, or, in rare cases, pure selfless love.

Outside your inner circle, there lies your **COMMUNITY CIRCLE**. People can belong to various communities and, as such, contribute to their development and thriving. It can be one's neighborhood, it can be an online forum for

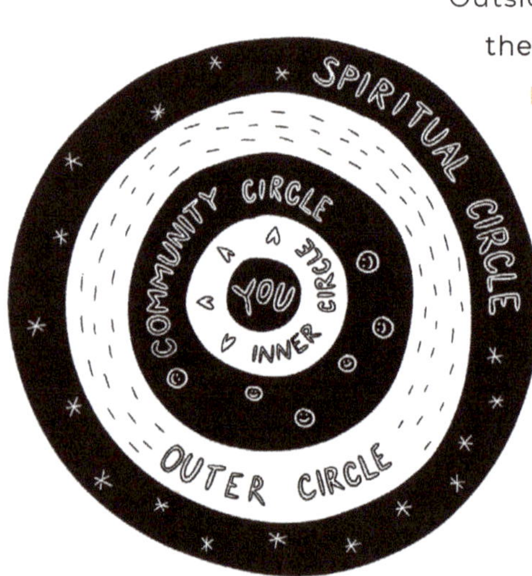

photography enthusiasts, a school class, colleagues at work, or a sports team, for example.

You can participate in these communities, or interact with them, both actively and passively, regardless of their location. For instance, if a French person donates to her favorite NGO in Afghanistan, she becomes part of its community as one of its supporters.

Beyond that, other humans we deal with belong to the OUTER CIRCLE, i.e., the category we could label as "the rest of the world." They can be important to us in one way or another, but our heart doesn't beat for them. We mostly don't feel responsible for their wellbeing or interests.

The last stratum, the SPIRITUAL CIRCLE, transcends all others. It affects human relationships and lives profoundly, although we tend to disregard its significance. It stands behind the force of our intuition, behind that special energy that gives birth to love, behind phenomena we call "miracles," behind occasions we like to dismiss as "coincidences."

Chance, destiny, the hand of God, mystery. We have many names for the moments in our lives we fail to make sense of or decipher by reason.

5. You're an Addict

There are more than seven billion people in the world. So where exactly is your place?

You and all other layers of your social reality are linked by a two-way channel. You affect people around you with your actions and words. They, in turn, affect you with theirs. It's as simple as that. Our efforts in life and work should then basically gravitate towards maximizing the positive impact we have on each other and minimizing the negative one.

Bear in mind this easy formula:

1. Amplify **THE POSITIVE IMPACT** on other people's lives and create value for them.

2. Cut down **THE NEGATIVE IMPACT** of other people's behavior and judgments on you.

In fact, whatever others say or do, albeit with the best of intentions, should not affect our core beliefs.

But wait, why not let other people play a part in my life? After all, I should be able to connect, learn, or accept appreciation.

It is, indeed, important to create bonds with others, share, and grow personally based on our experience and observations. Yet, as a matter of fact, what we don't need is their recognition in order to define who we are. It's us who over time make the PERCEPTION OF OUR SELF-ESTEEM AND WORTHINESS dependent on various signs of affection, appreciation, attention, approval, and acceptance.

We learn to judge ourselves through the eyes of other people. Appreciation is comforting, rejection hurts. Remember Pavlov's dogs?

Imagine each of these "A's" to be a sweet, highly addictive pill:

AFFECTION – "I like you."

APPRECIATION – "You're good."

ATTENTION – "I'm listening to you."

APPROVAL – "You're right."

ACCEPTANCE – "You're one of us."

The more we receive, the better it feels. When we're deprived of them, we would do anything to get them back.

When someone offers you this Sweet Pill, don't hesitate to accept it. Taste it, chew it, but don't swallow it every single time. Don't let it change who you truly are. Only if you reduce your addiction to a minimum can you REGAIN CONTROL OF YOUR SELF-ESTEEM, irrespective of what anyone else says or thinks about you.

6. Does Pain Beat Pleasure?

*M*ost of the time we yearn for affection and appreciation. Now and then, though, we face difficulties accepting them. We're afraid that we would end up disappointing the person who respects us. We feel unworthy of someone's kindness. Or we may be reluctant to return an act of generosity.

A person who feels **whole and worthy** is not needy, yet they know how to accept praise and say thank you.

On the other hand, we tend to apprehend disapproval, hostility, or rejection. Nevertheless, all too often we can't help ourselves when people serve us the Bitter Pill. We readily let it enter our bodies and poison our souls with harmful thoughts, and as a consequence with unhealthy emotions.

Negative thoughts: self-depreciation, imagining failure, self-judgment, judging others, blaming, developing catastrophic scenarios, bringing back unhappy memories, self-pity, doubts, worries, complaints... Just fill in the blanks.

It should be noted here that it's important for a person to recognize, accept, and express the whole range of emotions, not only the positive ones, since the role of an emotion is to send a signal that some of our needs are not being met, or that they are downright threatened. We may then call some emotions "negative" or even "unhealthy" when we fail to read their language and end up being miserable without channeling them into an action or a change.

But by now you've probably guessed the golden question. Why are we so keen to welcome the Bitter Pill, even though it makes us feel so bad? Why do we let negative thoughts fill our heads, indulging in them, multiplying them?

The answer is: We are steadfast in our conviction that we can defeat them!

We're prone to fighting the shadows of past words and actions. We like to pick up extinct conversations and incidents, and rewind them over and over in our heads. We analyze the words that have been uttered, we come up with better answers. We wake up unpleasant emotions, or even fabricate a set of brand new ones.

And somehow we're simultaneously hoping we will feel better in the end.

It's as if we tried treating overweight with overeating. It's satisfying for the time being, but eventually our body keeps suffering.

We tend to believe it's the other people who make us feel bad. But in fact it's our own mind that turns their actions and words into monsters that keep haunting us, waiting for us to accept the challenge, which we almost always do.

There's a murky boxing arena in your head. When you enter, you can see countless boxing rings spread all over the place. In each box, a fearsome opponent is impatiently waiting.

They fix their eyes on you, they beckon to you.

Adrenaline kicks in. You tremble with thrill. You choose the most formidable rival. You enter the ring.

And then you fight, and fight, and fight, you bleed, your bones get smashed, your flesh gets ripped. You get beaten to oblivion. You're left weakened, crippled, and even more susceptible to such futile duels.

Never accept the challenge. You cannot win.

7. Just Let Them Pass

When someone mocks your work, laughs at your dreams, or condemns your ideas, the crucial first step to protect yourself is AWARENESS. It may seem unnecessary since the whole situation is clearly unpleasant, but naming things helps.

Before you jump in to scrutinize your irksome feelings and fight your monsters, try to focus your mind on the plain fact that you're just being challenged. Nothing more.

> Words can hurt. They can turn into arrows that penetrate one's thin skin with their sharp tips. Yet, despite the momentary pain, a strong individual deliberately decides not to retaliate. And over time, the skin grows thicker and the arrows bounce off.

In most cases, people say or do things not to cause you pain specifically, but because they have their own issues to deal with. Their harmful acts and words often trace back to their own monster zoo they've been building up for years. And when some of the monsters break free, they tend to join the closest available menagerie.

Therefore, the second step is DISMISSAL.

While various thoughts and emotions are making their way in, you should acknowledge their message (e.g., *I feel angry, because this seems to be an attack on my self-worth*), instead of suppressing them right away, but afterward you should do your best to let them go.

Let them pass without giving them the attention they could feed off of. And when you don't listen, they subside as quickly as they appear.

So shall we not fight back when people treat us badly?

When someone keeps humiliating you, embarrassing you, or hurting you on purpose, there's little reason to keep them in your life. However, as mentioned earlier, the chances are that we simply hurt ourselves by something that is quite likely not that personal.

The best response might be a straightforward verbal formulation of your disapproval, with no emotions attached. It's okay to say, "I don't agree with you," or "Your behavior hurts me." It's less okay to get into an energy-draining argument with the other or, even worse, with yourself.

8. The Flashing Neons

We're born WHOLE and WORTHY.

However, as the time passes, our worthiness is challenged. We are deprived of affection. We lack attention. We're rejected by the ones we love. We face indifference, contempt, insecurity.

And then one day, huge neon signs start flickering in our heads:

Am I missing something?
Am I good enough?

They appear when we're about to make decisions. They make us uncomfortable. They blur our minds at the least appropriate moments.

The Sweet Pill (affection, appreciation, attention, approval, acceptance) and the Bitter Pill (rejection, indifference, depreciation, disapproval, hate) are usually fast weapons at hand.

The Sweet Pill makes them stop glaring. *I'm lovable! I have value! I belong!*

The Bitter Pill makes them shine so strong that we can't help ourselves but take on the fight with the thoughts and emotions they awaken.

If we aim to attain the desired state of wholeness and worthiness, we should resort to mental detoxification and reduce our addiction to both. Only when we can be content with ourselves as we truly are do we develop a healthy self-esteem.

You will feel pleasure. You will also feel pain. That's only natural.

> **Pleasure is the blow of fresh air. It keeps the flames of our courage and creativity burning.**
>
> **Pain is the detector of danger. Without pain we wouldn't be able to tell that there's something wrong.**

But neither pleasure nor pain should disrupt the whole system, your mind and your body. They shouldn't change who you are.

People who love you "unconditionally" are then your invaluable companions on the formidable journey of self-transformation. Those who accept you as you are can look at your genuine core and not ask for anything else. Keep them close and cherish their presence in your life. With them by your side, you will grow strong and bold.

9. Tear Down Those Walls

When we are born, our world doesn't have limits. Just about anything can happen, which is terrifying and exciting at once.

At first, little children work hard on figuring out what is going on around them. And they don't seem too unhappy about it because more information usually means less fun exploring. But not knowing at all may also lead to unpleasant surprises, suffering, and pain. That's why, little by little, their deep-rooted instinct of interpreting and labeling inevitably prevails.

Human nature dictates to seek security. The more we think we know about how the world works, the more protected we feel. Besides, the majority of people we connect or interact with, especially those who find some personal interest in our lives, tend to share their unique point of view, starting with our parents, teachers, or friends, along with our bosses, teammates, lovers, or even our rivals.

We are told what is good and bad. We get rewarded with attention and affection when we approve of other people's opinions. We are also purposely manipulated to serve the needs of others.

Starting in our childhood, we spend a large volume of our mental capacity on generating beliefs on how people are, how they think, what motivates them, why they behave in a certain way, why they treat us poorly, why they like us, why they don't like us, or what their hidden intentions might be.

We feel safe when we conclude that we have come to understand the general pattern. Knowing the rules shall give us ample space to adapt our behavior so that we are able to address our own problems and fill our own needs.

The danger lies in the singular representation of the world as we construct it within our minds and its unique set of principles by which we judge everything around us, and most notably ourselves. This world inevitably becomes our prison. We obey its order and trust its rules. What's more, we believe other individuals should follow them as well.

If you aspire to become an entrepreneur, make an effort to set yourself free. EMBRACE THE FACT THAT HOW YOU SEE THE WORLD IS A WORK OF FICTION. It may have assisted you in surviving until now, but it has possibly hindered not only your relationships with others but also your personal growth and creativity.

Keeping one's mind open means drilling holes into its surrounding wall so it can breathe and branch out.

Many people fail to do so because the wall looks impenetrable. It is cemented by historical beliefs and subjective assumptions. And since they are comfortable and safe within their small enclosures, they give up on learning about the precarious worlds of others.

They detest ideas that don't fit. They refuse to accept other people as they are. They wish everyone would change to their own image.

The world
is a vast and splendid
jungle that keeps
its finest treasures
deep and hidden
from those
who never dare

Nearly all individuals are bound by the borders of their fabricated worlds. However, these are connected by delicate fibers that represent our shared needs, values, or fears. Devote your time to tracking and recognizing these rare connections. Replace over-thinking with observing and impartial listening.

THE WORLD IS A VAST AND SPLENDID JUNGLE THAT KEEPS ITS FINEST TREASURES DEEP AND HIDDEN FROM THOSE WHO NEVER DARE. When you venture out of your shelter, you may get hurt, rather often than not, but if you do, you will see more than most other men and women ever do. You become a person of courage and character. A person who leads and innovates. An entrepreneur.

10. Wheelwork of the Universe

As an ambitious entrepreneur, you would want to if not change then at least improve the world around you. Needless to say, there's no better place to start than right there, at the very epicenter—with You.

You are certainly not the most important element of the universe. Actually, most probably you're a fairly minor particle. But just like anything else in nature, you have your role to play.

Unlike most other creatures on Earth, PEOPLE ARE UNIQUE IN THEIR PERPETUAL STRUGGLE TO REVEAL THE MEANING BEHIND THEIR EXISTENCE. We eat, drink, and poop to keep ourselves alive. We are capable of grasping how to reproduce. We take care of our offspring and normally even of each other. We create, build, and destroy things. We work, earn money, and buy stuff. Yet, many of us don't have a clue why and to what end.

Some make art to leave behind. Some try to pass the best of themselves on to their children. Some seek joy and adventure. Some choose suffering and pain. Some compete with others. Some compete with themselves. Some accumulate property. Some collect sexual partners.

Who is right? Who holds the right key?

As it seems, most organisms don't bother themselves with redundant existential questions. They do nothing but what is expected of them. They fit into their place on Earth like cogs into an elaborate wheelwork.

So again the question stands: What is the role of people here?

On the whole, we are destroying our planet at a massive pace. The Earth and most of the animals would be probably much relieved if we left them alone. But we do exist and there's a chance that we were brought to this world for some reason.

If you aim for your life to have value, you need to look much deeper than you've ever tried before.

THE ONLY FORCE THAT CAN MOVE YOU IN THE RIGHT DIRECTION IS YOUR OWN SPIRIT. It belongs to the paramount layer of our reality that connects us to everything else.

Intuition? God? Destiny? Maybe it has a name. Perhaps it doesn't matter at all.

Your mind and your spirit need to become close friends. Only then will you truly know yourself. Only then will you truly learn to know others.

How can your mind befriend your spirit? By learning to understand its language! For which there is no textbook. For which there is no trodden path.

Those quarreled siblings have been fighting for too long. One is profoundly wise and infinitely patient, one is stubborn, sometimes a bit shallow but extremely competent.

It takes a big deal of determination to make them reconcile. Keep trying. Force your mind to be attentive to her brother. Teach it to become trustful of her closest companion.

Once they start walking hand in hand, you will be able to get a taste of the special feeling when everything makes perfect sense. And with a smile on your face, you will remember those countless times in the past when you were fretting over your personal choices in life, when you were afraid to expose yourself and get hurt, or when you somehow expected that people would take you for a fool.

Back then, the withering uncertainty often made you give up. Now your mind finally listens. She is in peace. She is not afraid. Not anymore.

It feels good, very good, not to bear the burden of judging attitudes that keep stifling your life choices. When the idea of failure turns from a gargantuan canine into a barking puppy, you get to discover, piece by piece, how to improve yourself, and through your better self how to give value to those around.

Then, because you hear people's needs and meet them to solve their issues, you become important to them. They talk and listen to you and demand your presence, your skills, your knowledge, your service. You become vital. Your cogs set other wheels into motion. You fit into the wheelwork of the cosmos.

As an entrepreneur, your job is to be useful. It's that simple.

11. You in the First Place

If we understand entrepreneurship as a means to delivering value, we must realize that ALL STARTS AND ENDS WITH SELF-IMPROVEMENT.

When I improve not only my skills, but also my body, my mind, my inner harmony, and my relationships, I provide myself with certain long-lasting value. Simply put, I become a better person. A person who is, or is on the way to being, strong, competent, and well adapted to create value for others.

Maintaining a healthy lifestyle would then be the obvious and essential first step. Paradoxically, that's where many ambitious entrepreneurs fail. Often, they achieve material success and build prosperous companies, yet their physical constitution insidiously degenerates to the point where they are no longer able to lead a quality life. Or operate their businesses as effectively as they would wish to do. Besides, permanent pressure takes a heavy toll on their ability to adequately deal with stress without restoring to various medications, stimulants, or sedatives.

We hear those stories all the time. People suffering from exhaustion, depression, insomnia, eating disorders, alcoholism, drug abuse, chronic pain, hormonal imbalance, or cardiovascular diseases are a norm rather than an exception.

Stress develops into the normal, not abnormal, state. Mental and communication abilities suffer. Conflict becomes the common modus operandi. Pain never seems to leave.

> The most important part of your business is you. The key ingredient to your success is you. Also, sometimes the problem with your business is again you.
>
> Therefore, healthy body and balanced mind are your first and foremost instruments to build and run a sustainable enterprise. Far more important than smart ideas, money, or the right connections.
>
> Because even the most sophisticated ship loses its sense without a helmsman.

Yet, human beings are extremely resilient, so it's quite easy for them to ignore this fact for a while, sometimes for many long years. If you aim at the "plan, execute, and succeed" track—as fast as possible and at any cost—you still have high chances to make it. How fit you will be to lead, innovate, maintain essential relationships, or enjoy proceeds of your success and the related comfort, that's a question for you to answer yourself.

Business schools and formal entrepreneurial training programs rarely teach you how to take care of yourself. In the best case, they advise you to target the needs of your potential customers (which in itself is perfectly fine). A number of leads, increase in revenue, jobs created... these are all quantifiable. And sacrifices need to be made.

As a self-taught entrepreneur, you are driven to learn loads of things from scratch at an insane pace. You must prove yourself and move others to have faith in you. Hence, your personal wellbeing is habitually at the very bottom of your priorities list. You tend to conclude that every extra hour dedicated to sleep, sports, fun, friends, or even family is an hour lost at the expense of faster growth.

It's also possible that you are not able to tell what your body and mind need to function properly. If that's the case, then you should start working on it right now. Unless you learn to cater to your own, you will never be good at identifying basic needs of other people.

Or maybe you willingly pay no attention to your health and mental state, while firmly believing it's the right way to go. And hoping that one day you will be able to catch up. Remember, though, the longer you treat something with neglect, the harder it gets to repair the damage done.

> If you fuel your diesel car with gasoline, it won't take you far. If you drop your phone on a hard floor, it may never turn on again. If you spill hot coffee over your laptop, you may lose essential data.

All this sucks. But not as much as if it is your most vital working tool that turns defective.

TAKE CARE OF YOURSELF. ONLY THEN WILL YOU BE ABLE TO HELP OTHERS TOO. And helping others will in turn make you a better person and a much better entrepreneur.

12. Learning Is a Gift

*I*magine an infinite black wall that separates you from the rest of the world. There is only one pin-sized hole through which you can observe what is on the other side. You can't see much at the beginning, but every time you look, you learn something new and the hole gets a tad bigger.

It expands slowly, but the more you see, the more motivated you are to learn.

Every day you discover things to marvel at, and you can't get enough.

When you talk to people whose peepholes remain small, you struggle to understand each other. Sometimes they hate you. Often they listen to you because you come up with original ideas and solutions to their problems.

That's why you never stop learning. You want to keep broadening the horizons of your mind. If you stopped, the hole would start shrinking. And that would be the end.

The world is changing every second. But true NEURS LIKE TO ALWAYS STAY A FEW STEPS AHEAD. They are the ones who envisage what the future could look like. They keep their skills and knowledge up to date. They come up with new solutions to old problems. They approach difficult situations in innovative ways. And to avoid stagnation, they constantly foster their creative thinking.

You can master a new language or sport, you can learn to communicate better, you can improve your time management skills. There are no limits, whatsoever. Every new skill adds a new facet to your identity.

The satisfaction you may reach with material pleasures, on the other hand, is indeed limited. Even if you wake up tomorrow with a thousand times more money, it's unlikely that you will feel a thousand times happier. So we should not think about learning merely as an instrument to achieve a specific goal—to receive better grades or to attain a promotion. LEARNING IS A NURTURING PROCESS THAT HELPS YOU GROW FROM A TEENY WRINKLED SEED TO A STOUT AND GRACEFUL TREE.

The greatest gift of life is that we can become whoever we want to be, at any age. And the best thing is that we don't need anyone's sanction.

13. I Want vs. I Need

To build a great business, we need to give value.

Why? What does it even mean?

When you give value, you make someone's life better. You solve their problem. You provide what they want. You offer what they need.

Our needs range from the basic, PHYSICAL ones (food, water, air, sleep, sex, warmth, safety...), to EMOTIONAL (affection, attention, empathy, security, pleasure, esteem...), SOCIAL (communication, sharing, belonging, recognition...), INTELLECTUAL (learning, creativity, problem-solving...), and SPIRITUAL (faith, hope, love, harmony, purpose...).

Sometimes people know precisely what they want. Sometimes they have no clue. But they always have needs. Although they often struggle with formulating exactly what these needs are.

Take a man who desires the latest model of a sports car and is willing to pay a hefty price. On the surface, it may seem that he doesn't really need it. There are two others in his garage, and we conclude that he is simply a vain show-off. Yet, there is always a need lurking at the rear. What he needs may be acceptance by his peers (social need). It may be pure pleasure from driving faster than ever (emotional need). It may be attention from attractive women (emotional and social need). It can be sense of accomplishment (emotional need).

Or take a woman who donates all her savings to a charity in Uganda that delivers free lunches to primary schools. Some may admire her for being a noble altruist. Some may sneer at her for being crazy. If we ask her, she will respond, "I just wanted to help!" Then, we may dig deeper and discover that she has always lacked a sense of purpose in her life (spiritual need). Her self-esteem is also not the most solid. Deep inside, she is thirsty for approval and acknowledgment of her good deeds (emotional and social need). All in all, her act of philanthropy will make a few children less hungry (physical need).

PEOPLE HAVE NEEDS. AND WE ALL POSSESS CERTAIN KNOWLEDGE, SKILLS, AND ABILITIES TO FULFILL THOSE NEEDS. By doing so, we not only improve the world around us, we become more efficient and successful in our work and business activities too.

So work with this. Identify a specific need that is shared by a sizable proportion of the population. Deliver a product or service that directly satisfies this particular need. And finally, make such product or service better, less expensive, or more accessible than any of its substitutes.

Sustainable businesses focus on creating value, which in turn means improving people's lives and having a positive social impact. That's why good entrepreneurs listen and observe. They don't always give people what they want. They do their best to meet their needs.

14. Almighty Triumvirate

When you accept the fact that the world you have created in your head is not real and that any obstacles that prevent you from being successful in life are those you have fabricated yourself, many doors will begin opening in front of you. New solutions, new opportunities. Newly found inner harmony.

You wake up every day determined to work on yourself so that you can lead a fulfilling life and help others improve their own. You keep your eyes and ears open to make your thoughts and emotions work for you, not against you. You slowly get rid of the garbage you have accumulated over the years—the false presumptions, beliefs, and grievances that hinder your reasoning, spur harmful emotions, and all in all hurt your soul as such.

All three major parts that constitute your being (body, soul, spirit) are inseparably linked. IF THE SOUL SUFFERS, THE BODY IS ILL, AND THE SPIRIT MUTED.

When you manage to control your thoughts and emotions, your body becomes naturally healthier and stronger, often much more so than by using some miracle pills or various medical treatments. When you start ignoring limitations you've imposed on yourself, your spirit will awaken to help you live up to your potential. And having these three working in unison, you will not only reveal but also feel what your purpose as a human is.

Purpose is the most important thing to encounter within your lifetime, besides love. Love makes you feel worthy and connected. PURPOSE GIVES TRANSCENDENT MEANING TO YOUR ACTIONS.

Both purpose and love are manifestations of one thing: "I belong."

When we experience these two, our life makes sense. Our decisions, choices, even our mistakes. And whatever we build doesn't hinge on success or failure. It has its definitive purpose in itself. It brings value, to both ourselves and society.

The concordance of our individuality and our reality stands on four pillars:

Learning
Value
Purpose
Belonging

We learn, we develop, we grow. The better we are, the better we help others grow. And the more we give, the more we receive.

When we tap into our purpose, our knowledge, skills, and energy help us achieve exactly what we need and what we want.

15. Temet Nosce

*A*s an entrepreneur, you aspire to:

➡ **Actively shape your journey to success.**

➡ **Avoid being a victim of external circumstances.**

A company can't operate efficiently if its management is in shambles. You can't be in control of your life, or anyone else's for that matter, if you don't hold the reins of your own mind.

STEP 1:

Learn to become aware of toxic thoughts when they start plaguing your mind. It's not hard for you to take notice when you suffer from a headache, muscle pain, or fever, for instance. Also, normally, you don't blame people around for your symptoms.

Bad thoughts trigger unpleasant emotions. Unpleasant emotions in turn encourage bad thoughts. And you can have control over both. So **TREAT NEGATIVE THOUGHTS AND EMOTIONS JUST LIKE ANY OTHER SYMPTOM**. Assume ownership of the condition. Observe how it affects you with a healthy dose of distance and detachment.

It may take days, weeks, or even months, before you make this a routine practice, but it is exceptionally worth it. Being able to quickly recognize the first warning signs is the precursor to successful elimination of the disease.

STEP 2:

Our thoughts originate from the seemingly random particles of information that pass through our head in any given moment. It's entirely up to us which one of them we pick, charge with our positive, neutral, or negative judgment, materialize with our focus, and keep alive with our energy.

You know what happens when you examine yourself too eagerly once feeling unwell. Before long, it seems as if your symptoms have multiplied. You are frightened that you have developed a serious illness. And even if that's not the case, such stress you brought upon yourself can make your fears a reality.

Stick to the fact that ANY NEGATIVE THOUGHT, IF DULY IGNORED, AND ANY UNPLEASANT EMOTION, IF DULY UNDERSTOOD, FADES PROPORTIONALLY WITH TIME.

STEP 3:

Aim at achieving inner balance by RECONCILING YOUR MIND AND EMOTIONS (SOUL) WITH YOUR PHYSICAL WELL-BEING (BODY), AND METAPHYSICAL CONGRUENCE (SPIRIT).

Mens sana in corpore sano. A healthy mind resides in a healthy body.

Choose your thoughts. Breathe, sleep, exercise, drink enough water, eat less, and eat well. That's a simple, yet the most powerful, recipe for accumulating a huge amount of usable energy. Only if you preserve energy will you be able to see and understand where you are heading and why.

STEP 4:

As soon as you regain control over yourself, you can work on your relationships with other human beings.

People affect each other with words and actions. You are in control if you REDUCE THE DEPENDENCE OF YOUR SELF-ESTEEM ON WHAT OTHERS THINK OR SAY ABOUT YOU. You are in control if your perception of your worthiness and wholeness remains steadfast regardless of how others treat you, be it good (affection, appreciation, attention, approval, acceptance) or bad (hate, depreciation, indifference, disapproval, rejection).

Such control can be accomplished exclusively by exploring, understanding, and respecting your own value.

STEP 5:

As long as you genuinely honor your qualities and abilities, you're in full control of how other people see you.

> **You can fake confidence (I'm capable), but you can't fake self-esteem (I'm worthy).**

IF YOU BELIEVE IN YOUR CAPACITY TO SUCCEED, IT WILL INEVITABLY REFLECT IN YOUR APPEARANCE, POSTURE, GESTURES, TONE OF VOICE, WORDS, AND ACTIONS. This belief will then infect others, who will naturally assist you in paving your way to success.

Even better, if you develop a healthy sense of worthiness, you can eliminate any negative impact of other people's behavior on your mindset and resolve.

STEP 6:

Opportunities seldom arrive at your door by themselves. You and only you are responsible for actively shaping favorable circumstances and making the right choices. However, this would be hardly possible if you didn't know WHAT EXACTLY YOU WANT.

Here, try to be as specific as possible.

More money, more customers, more free time… or less stress, less annoying people, less insecurity?

No, not like that.

These can be your starting points for self-exploration but not a final answer. Go into as much detail as possible, and make your desired situation or goal somehow measurable (e.g., by degree, amount, etc.). Only then will you be able to tell when you have achieved it. Only once it becomes ingrained in your mind will you start moving in the right direction.

Imagine the pilot of the plane you're sitting on has received a set of obscure, confusing, and contradictory flight directions. Would you be confident that he will be able to stay on the right trajectory?

STEP 7:

Opportunities, money, and other resources you need to prosper are abounding. It's up to you to extend your hand.

One thing is extremely limited, though. Time. You can't buy it. You can't steal it. You can't capture it. Time is finite, within one's lifespan. The time you lose is irretrievable.

Time is the most squandered commodity on Earth.

We're all guilty of wasting it phenomenally, day by day.

It's about "the right time" you started TREATING TIME AS YOUR MOST VALUABLE RESOURCE. If you wish to run a thriving business, you need to know how to manage not only financial but physical and human resources competently. Yet, unless you recognize the full worth of the modest time allowance you were given at birth, you're not in control of anything.

STEP 8:

The occurrence of the right opportunities for achieving your goals goes hand in hand with DEDICATED PERSONAL GROWTH. For that reason, knowing what you want to achieve is a necessary but not sufficient condition for hitting your target.

Learning is the essence of progress in anything you do. It's not a privilege of a few. It gives you control over how the journey from where you are now to where you want to be will look like.

TIME
IS
THE MOST
SQUANDERED
COMMODITY
ON EARTH

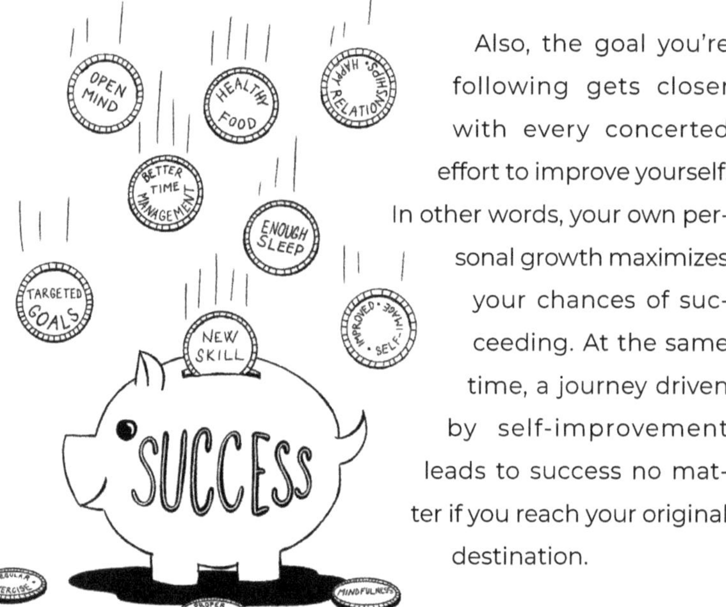

Also, the goal you're following gets closer with every concerted effort to improve yourself. In other words, your own personal growth maximizes your chances of succeeding. At the same time, a journey driven by self-improvement leads to success no matter if you reach your original destination.

Every step on the road to BETTER ME means dropping one coin in the piggy bank called SUCCESS.

16. Stop Being a Victim

*E*ntrepreneurs are not only capable of actively shaping their way to success. They AVOID FALLING VICTIM TO UNFAVORABLE CIRCUMSTANCES as well.

There are many things we can't change. For example, we can't change personalities of other people. Often, we have limited influence on how they decide to treat us. We can't predict everything that happens on a given day. And we certainly can't stop time.

However, all this doesn't mean that we are facing the world utterly exposed and vulnerable. It also doesn't mean that we should let just any external force determine who we are and how we feel.

EVEN THOUGH WE CAN'T CONTROL ALL THAT GOES ON IN OUR LIFE, WE CAN CONTROL BOTH OUR INNER AND OUTER RESPONSE. We can regulate our thoughts and, ergo, our emotions. We ourselves choose how to act and behave. And ultimately, we have the power to prevent most circumstances from having a lasting impact on our health, mental state, wellbeing, relationships, and personal growth.

Events or situations that are less than ideal in our eyes tend to spark off adverse thoughts, which in turn manifest in our bodies as debilitating emotions.

But what if we simply changed our subjective judgment?

Few events, situations, actions, or uttered words are inherently negative. Its us who evaluate them, who make a judgment, or an assumption. In a fraction of a second, our mind transforms a neutral "nothing" into a negative "something"—a problem.

Instead of dealing with problems as they come, we must decide how we like to experience what happens to us. Words are potent tools, and they shape our reality, not only when we say them out loud. Whatever we tell ourselves forges a new pattern in our mind and affects our further reasoning.

Ask yourself: Can I alter the circumstances? Can I control or influence what is happening?

NO ➡ Do I know someone who can?

YES ➡ I pass the issue to that person to deal with it, or I ask for help.

NO ➡ Either I let it be, not to waste any more of my scarce energy, or I carefully choose what judgment I make.

It is a problem only if I call it a problem.

YES ➡ Can I change it now?

YES ➡ Either I do it as soon as possible, or I let it be for good.

NO ➡ I do my best to release it from my mind until that moment comes.

Most destructive thoughts wake up the victim in us. Forgetting and forgiving equal not being a victim anymore.

17. Orchard

A child woke up.

Something was wrong.

She looked around, having difficulties to remember how she had gotten to where she was in the first place.

It seemed bleak and hopeless.

A ramshackle hut, surrounded by stones, dirt, and a few scattered shrubs. No road. No hills. No living being in sight. No sun behind the carpet of indifferent clouds.

A thick mist of loneliness shrouded her soul.

She stood up and headed out. Without a trustworthy plan or an agenda, but with a nagging sensation that she was not supposed to be there, that she was not supposed to feel that way.

Was it that she was not a child anymore? Could it be?

She felt aged. And almost unbearably tired. Resigned.

Children are curious and lighthearted. They see only the possible. Often, they like to act somewhat cheeky. They resent "no's," and they always try to find their way around to reach at what they want.

She began marching.

Actually, when she thought about it, it used to be quite easy to point her little finger and say, loud and clear, "I want this!"

She glanced at her hands. They looked much bigger, wrinkled, and… restless.

They say eyes are windows to one's soul. She believed that hands may reveal a lot as well. She had known a person with impenetrable looks but kind hands. And she had known one with a warm gaze, yet treacherous handshake.

Before she could realize she was walking in a circle, a bird appeared on the horizon.

What feathers!

It was the most gorgeous thing she had ever seen.

Proud ultramarine for its grace. Mellow daffodil for its peacefulness. Bold crimson for its willpower. Zippy chartreuse for its individuality.

A sting of jealousness pierced her hard. Immediately, she felt ashamed.

The bird gave the impression of a creature whose sole purpose is to exist and be beautiful.

There was a swelling pressure under her rib cage while her soul was attracted to join the soul of the bird and fly away.

The stones and the shrubs heard the child's soul screaming. Not so much the child herself. She had lost her ability to hear the fundamental sounds of nature a long time ago.

All of a sudden, the bird disappeared as fast as it had appeared. Her soul sunk back and fell silent.

She went back to shuffling along.

"What are you doing?"

She jumped a little in surprise and turned back. The bird was right there again, above her head. It was sitting on a lush, blooming tree.

This tree... how could she miss it?

Hesitantly, she replied:

"I'm walking."

"Where to? If I may ask."

"I'm not so sure."

"Then why are you walking? Why don't you sit and rest?"

"I don't like it here."

"What don't you like?"

"I don't know. Look around. What's there to like?"

"I think it's wonderful here. Every day, when I wake up, I feel infinitely grateful. And to be frank with you, if I didn't, if I lost this feeling of gratitude, I'm not sure if I would ever be able to fly up again."

"You are crazy... But you're a beautiful bird," she added hastily not to offend.

"Why do you think I'm crazy?"

"Pardon me. I meant... it's a barren land. No one lives here, nothing grows here."

"I live here. And you too! And what about this marvelous tree?" it chirped.

"I have never noticed this tree before," the child uttered almost accusingly. "Anyway, I have always stayed in this place, I suppose. Where else would I go?"

"If you don't like it here, then go somewhere where you would like it better. That's fairly simple."

She thought about that for a few long seconds. While doing so, her expression fluently transformed from confused to resolved.

"And how do I get to such a place? As you can see for yourself, there are no roads whatsoever. How can I find my way? I'm sure you have traveled to all four corners of the world. Can you advise me?"

The words came gushing out of her like out of a burst water pipe.

"You're right. I have seen more than you could ever imagine... until now," the bird proclaimed.

She spotted a somewhat reassuring glimmer in its dreamy eyes.

And then, a weird thing happened. Something tore inside her. The part of her that was dominated by reason exposed its true face and laughed maniacally at her for listening to a talking bird.

However, quite simultaneously, the child's spirit slowly awakened from a very deep sleep.

"I can't give you good advice, though," continued the bird.

The child couldn't bear the crushing laughter of her mind and spit out:

"I knew it! You were just trying to trick me... with your magical trees and whatnot."

"I have never said that this tree is magical. Don't be angry with me just because you can't see things and I do."

"I do see the damn tree. But it had not been here until you sat on it. That's for sure," the child snapped.

"Very well, then. Let's make an experiment," the bird replied and flew off.

The tree didn't move.

After a while, the bird returned and perched graciously on its preferred branch.

"You see? The moment you believed this tree existed, you broke the spell. Before, you had never thought about such a tree. You didn't dream about it. And when you saw one, you didn't like it.

"I mean... you did like the tree. You even admired it. But you were not comfortable with the idea of this tree standing here. What if it was just an illusion? What if you woke up tomorrow and it was gone?

"Every morning, you would welcome the day with no colors, no life around, no joy. You had learned how to cope with all that. Although you sensed it was not right, you didn't know any better.

"But now you know better. To have a tree is better than to not have a tree. It provides shade. It makes a relaxing sound when the wind moves through its branches. Its leaves change color to mark the different phases of the year. And who knows? Maybe, when the spring comes, it may bear fruit for you to eat.

"Isn't it a wonderful thing, a tree?"

The child sat down on the dusty ground and crossed her legs. Her head was spinning. A colorful, talking bird and a tree that may bear fruit, all in one single day. It was a lot to take in.

The bird went on:

"Even if someone came tonight, cut the tree, and dragged it away, the image of it would remain in your head. Moments might come when you would question your sanity. It's possible that you would even come to believe this tree was a mere fancy, a product of your dreams. But you would always know that to have a tree is better than to not have a tree."

The child weighed the words of her new feathered friend. She listened to the leaves rustling. She let the wind stroke her cheeks and ruffle her hair.

The bird was right. It was good to have a tree.

"How do you know the tree will be here tomorrow?"

The bird chuckled.

"It's been here for years. You have passed by it countless times. I sit here every day. It's my favorite tree!"

"But I have never seen you. Why? Why have you never said anything?"

"Oh boy, I did! And I sing. The tree rustles. The wind whispers. The stones murmur their ancient wisdoms. The shrubs like to catch the dirt... There is so much life here. You didn't see it because it didn't fit with the image you had of the world around you. You were convinced it's the only one, and the right one."

"Now, there's a tree and a bird in my world!" the child exclaimed.

"Correct. And there can be more. Or less. It's all up to you... So do you still feel like leaving?"

The spirit of the child was by now in full force. It filled every cell of her body with its balmy and tender presence.

Her mind calmed down. She was at peace. And her heart was beating drums of quiet celebration.

She pushed herself up. When she looked at her hands in the mud, albeit dirty, they seemed a bit smaller and softer than before.

"You know, don't take me wrong. I like you and I like your tree. But when I was sitting, I thought that such a beautiful tree certainly needed plenty of water. It seldom rains here. What if I went to find a stream or a river, so I can water its thirsty roots?"

"Why do you ask me? I'm just a bird who likes to sing. I've told you before that I can't tell you what to do or where to go."

The child sighed.

"You're one cranky…" she stopped herself. "Well, then, I'm leaving anyway. I will look for some water, so that the tree can live longer, and I can sit in its shadow, and listen to its leaves rustling."

She turned away and began to walk.

"Hey, wait!"

"What?!"

The child stopped and flashed back her petulant face.

"You'll get lost. Let me tell you how to find the road."

"Are you joking?! You've told me twice that you couldn't help me."

"I couldn't give you any advice because you were not sure where you wanted to go. So I didn't know how to help you.

"It's still good that you asked, though.

"Some people pass by, stop, and talk to me for hours, complain about their woes, but never ask for help.

"You did ask. However, you just wanted something vaguely different, something vaguely better. Just like everyone else!

"People often build a bizarre double prison for themselves. On one hand, they create a framed painting of their world whose bounds they refuse to cross. On the other hand, they spend their lives longing for something or someone to come and set them free.

"They don't realize that seeking something 'better' is a trap our life has prepared for us. It's a chimera that dwindles away when you approach it and disappears entirely once you touch it.

"Today, you've discovered new things because you had changed. You woke up with a trickle of energy, a feeling, an idea that you can do something. Anything.

"Then you made your first step. A series of steps, in fact. And even this meager force made you see me, and you saw my tree.

"Before, life gave you exactly what you wanted. Although you didn't like what you had, you didn't ask for more. You see? That's another trap people fall into. They think they want a lot from life. Yet in truth, they're afraid to ask too much. They perpetually sabotage their own happiness. They're like a leaky bottle that can never be filled."

The child tried hard to remember what she had asked from life in the past. She wanted to tell the bird about all the things she had ever desired and never received. But those memories had already melted into one amorphous lump of bitterness and disappointment.

As if it was reading her mind, the bird sang out:

"But this is past now!

"Remember that you should never chase Past. He and his brother Future have been cursed to always run in the opposite directions so they can never meet. That's why they incessantly fight for your attention, to avoid loneliness in their predicament. Only the third brother, Present, stands in between. Quiet and timid.

"Past is the most charming of them all. He is a master of seduction and flattery! Rarely does someone resist his courting. Yet, his only goal is to drag you along and make you his personal slave. He has already amassed a loyal army of lackeys and instructed them to recruit fresh members day by day.

"Future is a lone warrior and a bit of a show-off. Many line up to stand in awe and observe his skill and prowess. Yet, they often fail to approach and befriend him either out of fear of hearing 'no,' or out of fear of being hacked to pieces.

"Present is a shy sage with a tranquil gaze. He has so much to tell and so much to teach, whereas people dismiss him for being an annoying bore. If only they knew that the secret to happiness is to stop still and listen. Unlike his brothers, he wants you to stay free and in harmony with the world."

The bird flew one large circle, as if to emphasize its words, and descended onto the child's shoulder. There it whispered its final words of advice:

"Do you see that cross-shaped cairn there on the horizon? It's an old navigation landmark for pilgrims. You will see many others on your way. Follow them and you will find your spring."

The child stood speechless. She had spotted those objects before, but it had never occurred to her that they were anything more than random piles of stones.

When she turned to offer her thanks, the bird was already mounting the clouds in jubilation of the present day.

Once again, she felt a pinch of envy. If only she could be so lighthearted.

She made up her mind! She would look ahead to learn courage from Future, while keeping company to Present, who would show her beautiful things just as the bird did.

For many days, she walked. She tracked the stacks of stones. She contemplated the land's scenery during the day. She talked to the stars at night.

At first, the stars didn't respond. But the child didn't give up. She told them about all the things she had seen since she left her home. The grass she had slept on, the bugs she had tried not to crush, the warm wind that had caressed her skin. She told them about her hut. She told them about going to bed without a kiss on her forehead. She told them about having a friend whose feathers were so bright that it hurt her eyes.

One night the stars put their luminous heads together and agreed that the child had grown wise enough to understand what they had to say. For a fraction of a second, they shone a little brighter to extend affirmation of their friendship.

They assured her that she was not alone. And then they asked her if she wished to learn the secret to happiness.

The child responded that she had already learned the secret to happiness. The bird taught her. She simply needed to hang around with Present and learn what he had to share.

As it takes many years for the light of the stars to reach the Earth, they didn't know who Present was.

They knew Dark, though, who terrifies most human beings, especially the small ones.

The stars grew fond of the girl so they decided to reveal their secret to her. The secret they had been passing to each other for millions of years.

They told her that Dark couldn't exist without Light. They told her that Dark and Light were manifestation of the same thing, two halves that made a whole, and they were always in perfect balance.

They told her if she was ever to feel despair sneaking into her heart, she should remember the night sky. For it wasn't alive until the stars broke its blackness. And for there was no despair without hope. And no problem without a solution.

How lucky she was.

As if centuries have passed since the day she woke up forlorn and decided to walk away, her steps as heavy as her mind. And still, it took so little for her to learn how to see beauty in any place she passed by. What's more, it took only one conversation with the stars for her to understand that darkness didn't exist without the promise of light.

Chatting with the stars also helped the child ignore the unpleasant tiny voices in her own head. They hissed at her that she should have never left her home, that she should have never listened to that flying animal, and that if she kept walking, she would inevitably fail.

Luckily, she could tell by now that they were the servants of Past, and she made every effort to steer away from them.

She was afraid though. That was the truth. She had never been that far, and she hadn't the slightest idea what awaited her on the journey she so daringly embarked on. Future was quite an intimidating fellow. She didn't feel quite ready yet to join him on the battlefield. For the time being, she had settled to cautiously keep an eye on him from a distance.

Present, on the other hand, proved to be a true friend. With every day, the roadside grew greener, the sky gleamed bluer, and the sun shone warmer. She was slowly learning that for the grass to sprout, she needed to appreciate the softness of its stalks, for the sky to protect her head, she needed to know all the shapes of its clouds and count all its many hues, and for the sun to shine, she needed to bow and greet her with gratitude and humility.

Soon, she realized that much like Past boasted his own personal army of saboteurs, Present was accompanied by a legion of loyal disciples whose mission was to help his friends in any way possible. She just had to keep looking.

On the seventh day, she was famished and thirsty. She had found a dozen cairns by then, but none of them led her to a river, a stream, or even a teeny spring. On the verge of giving up, she remembered the words of the bird, who said that one needs to dream about things for them to become real.

You simply let them become a part of your world.

She also remembered the tree the bird liked to sit on. It stood not far from her home. For a long time, it had been invisible, until one day it was visible. And it made her set off on this peculiar journey.

She didn't want to make the same mistake twice. If she came to believe that she was going to starve to death, it was likely to happen.

The bird was right. She had changed. She preferred to see the world as a garden of opportunity, not a jungle of obstacles.

And so she knew that a solution would come soon.

One morning, she heard a familiar rustle. Where was it coming from?

She sat on the ground, took a few deep breaths, and let her soul seek advice of her spirit. Upon short deliberation, they told her to stay still and pay attention to the sounds of nature.

And so she did.

Before long, she recognized the calling. The calling of the magnificent tree she had left at home.

She sprung up and wandered around. After a short while, she spotted a low rusty gate grown over with bushes. Cautiously, she pushed the cold metal back with both her hands, now stronger than ever.

Behind the gate, an orchard was hiding, from the eyes of those who didn't see.

The place looked as if a living soul had not set a foot there for ages. The grass was tall and taken over by weeds. To her delight, the trees appeared to be bejeweled with plump and inviting fruits. Fragrant, juicy. And only hers.

They whispered to her. They knew why she came, and they invited her for a feast.

She eagerly reached out to one that was hanging low enough for her to grab.

"Be careful, not all of them are ready to eat."

The child froze in place. She looked around but didn't see anyone.

"Here, here, little lady," a mischievous voice croaked at her.

The child cut through the grass until she caught sight of a giant mossy stump.

"Was it you?" the child asked without a trace of surprise in her voice. She had already talked to a bird and to the stars.

She had learned that there were many things that speak to us if only we open our ears wide enough.

"Here, here!"

The child came closer and saw a crevice in the stump. Inside, two hazel eyes were peering out at her.

"Hello. Are you stuck there?"

"Oh no, little lady, this is my home. Are you alone?" inquired the funny voice.

"Yes, I'm on my own."

"Have you seen any people around? People with axes, saws, nets?"

"I haven't seen any people with such things. Or without. I have been walking for several days and haven't met a single human being. Are you a human?"

"You don't beat around the bush! I like that."

The eyes lightened up the darkness with laughter. And then the girl knew that it didn't matter if the creature hiding in the stump's cavity was human or otherwise. Eyes that laugh candidly and crackle with humor can be trusted with life.

A short figure wriggled out of its humble dwelling. It was indeed a human being! Female human being. Very, very old.

"It is nice meeting you," the child politely greeted the old woman.

"My pleasure, my pleasure, little lady. Please, have a seat," the woman pointed to a large boulder lying nearby.

When the child sat down, it occurred to her that the stone had somewhat of an odd shape. If you focused long enough, you could almost imagine it to have the features of a screaming face.

"Now, tell me, little lady, why are you here?"

The child was ravenous and found it hard to concentrate. At the same time, it was nice to share a couple of words with someone who may become her soulmate.

"I live alone, many days of walking from here. I'm looking for a stream, or a river, or a spring to water my tree."

"You have a tree?"

"Well, it's not my tree. It's a tree that grows close to the hut where I live. For a long time it had been invisible, until one day it was visible."

"An invisible tree! Tell me more, please. I like trees!" the woman was begging her with a keen, toothless smile.

"I like trees too! There used to be no tree where I live, and I didn't even want one, to be frank with you. I had never dreamt about it. I only dreamt about living at a nicer place. I didn't know what this place should look like though. So my dreams never really came true."

"Until you saw an invisible tree!"

The woman's body was fidgeting with excitement.

"Not precisely. Until one morning when I felt that there was nothing I could do except for taking a few steps ahead. I didn't know back then where I was heading, but it seemed right to do something small rather than to do nothing at all.

"And then a bird flew over my head."

"A bird? A bird! Was he invisible as well?"

The child glanced askew at the woman. She began to question her mental health. After all, she lived in a tree stump.

"No!" the child growled. "How could I have seen the bird if it were invisible?

"It was entirely visible and beautiful.

"The bird told me that my world could be much more colorful, even as colorful as its gorgeous feathers. I could paint anything I wanted into my world."

"You are a painter. An artist!" the women cried out.

"Yes, in a way," the child replied patiently. "My mind is a canvas without a frame and I can paint anything I want onto that canvas. And then if I keep my eyes and my ears open, I will see and hear the things I have painted happening."

"You must have painted marvelous things! I would love to see them."

"Not yet, but every day, I add something small. Something new. I've made new friends, and I've learned many things in the past few days."

"Very well, little lady. And what about that invisible tree?"

The woman had lived alone for many long years, and the only thing she wanted in that moment was a good story. And the only thing the child wanted in that moment was one bite of juicy fruit.

Two solitary creatures, sitting in the midst of an enchanted orchard.

They both knew what they were there for. They both had it within their reach. And they were in no rush.

"The bird has its favorite tree it likes to sit on. I had passed by them many times, but I didn't see anything because my canvas was too small. There was not enough space for a blooming tree and a colorful bird.

"Then why did you leave?

"It is better to have a tree than to not have a tree. You are surrounded by many. But there is only one close to my home.

Now that I have found it, I don't want to lose it again. That's why I decided to look for water. Every tree needs water.

"Yes, trees need water, and they also need sun and air. Your tree most probably gets water from the ground, otherwise it would be long dead.

"Also, you're very far from your home. Even if you found a water stream, how would you carry the water back? In your hands?" the good-hearted woman smiled again.

The child was somewhat offended and her soul sank. There she was, exhausted from a long walk, and that woman was telling her that it was all for nothing.

"That's easy for you to say. You live in the midst of trees that bear juicy fruit."

"Believe me, it's not easy for me to talk about trees. This orchard used to be a home to hundreds and hundreds of various trees. In the spring, the smell oozing from their flowers would cross oceans and reach even the most distant islands.

"However, although the fruits were feeding dozens of families far and around, their delicacy was unbearable for many people.

"But that's a story for another day. Let's have a look at your problem first. You can't water your tree all by yourself."

"So what should I do? I have walked for so many days, for nothing!"

"What do you mean, for nothing? When you spoke about painting your world with beautiful things, about making new friends, were you just bragging?

"I'm not sure you have learned anything, my dear."

The child felt as if those reproachful words came from the skies above, not from the woman's mouth. She looked up to make sure the bird was not fluttering somewhere around.

It wasn't. The stars were sleeping too.

"Whether you return home with or without water doesn't really matter. Mother Nature will take care of your tree. Don't worry about that.

"The important thing is that you have come all the way until here. You would have never left your hut if you hadn't chosen a goal to follow. You cared about it deeply, which made you move forward, despite all the obstacles, despite you being on your own, thirsty, and hungry.

"And along the way, your spirit, a powerful force, woke up to give you guidance and protection."

The child has long embraced that warm feeling around her heart, which appeared the day she spoke with the talking bird. It gave her courage to do things she had never tried before.

The woman stood up and picked an apple, which looked completely ordinary but was ready to eat. She offered it to the child and continued:

"This force has a remarkable ability to bring us to the right place at the right time. It is extremely fragile, though. Much like your tree, it requires plenty of space and fresh air. It needs to be fueled by curiosity, learning, and imagination. It stems from our hearts and is kindled through our nose when we breathe, through our eyes when we observe, and through our ears when we listen.

"The imagination of people when they are little is wild and boundless. And then a terrible thing happens.

"They're told that their world is out of their control. They're told what their world should look like. They're told they need to follow many different rules to fit into that world.

"And they get scared. They are scared of being alone, of being rejected. They don't want to be left out of a painting someone had drawn for them, as you have mentioned before. So they voluntarily step into its frame."

"What happens to their spirit then?"

"Their spirit weakens, and people forget that they were once in charge of their destiny."

"The bird told me that life gives us exactly what we ask it for. Have you always got what you wanted?"

"Not always. Mainly because I didn't want those things from the core of my heart.

"That's how we people are. We often spend a great deal of time running after something which we believe will make us more satisfied, happier. Sometimes, we bestow all our hopes on one magical solution to all our problems.

"Whether we reach it or not, we realize after a while that the world has remained the same, that we ourselves have remained the same. And we look back at all the time that has passed, and our heart weeps because it knows that this time has been lost forever.

"That's why you should always choose carefully what you wish for. And that's why this orchard has been almost destroyed.

"Let me tell you something..."

There was a palpable hesitation in the woman's voice. She smiled nervously once again, and her short fingers straightened the rim of her skirt, her eyes firmly pinned to the child's face.

"Some of these trees are not ordinary trees. Their fruit can in fact make your wishes come true."

"Really?!"

"There's a catch, though." One elfin finger raised itself in admonition.

While the child was listening, she caught a glimpse of her own hands. They were smooth, warm, and firm. Just as the hands of a child should be.

"Once you eat it, you cannot take your wish back. You have to deal with what you have cooked for yourself. And that's what people don't realize. That only they themselves are in charge of their lives. Nothing or no one can change how they feel and what they experience.

"That's why you should never get what you want too easily. The roads that lead to your dreams must be lined with pitfalls, and that shall demand all your powers. Only then will you think twice if it's worth your time and all the things you need to give up along the way. Only then will you learn to appreciate what may await you in the end. Only then will you get to taste what it feels like to be truly fulfilled.

"Our job, mine and my family's, has been to protect the orchard from people, and protect people from the orchard. Unfortunately, we failed. The desire of people to get what they want fast and without pain is impossible to fight.

"Eventually, the rumors would spread and they would come. One by one. They would ask to buy fruits from the wish trees. When we refused, they would steal them anyway.

"And then one day, they would come for revenge."

"What are you talking about? Why revenge? Your fruit made their wishes come true, didn't it?"

The woman sighed.

"Oh, my little lady, it's not about what you wish for but what your ultimate intention is.

"People believe, for example, that their life would change for the better if only they had plenty of money. They want to become rich. Then, when they finally do, instead of enjoying the freedom money gives a man to do good things for others and himself too, they spend it carelessly and without consideration. In the end, they often become less happy than they had been before.

"Or they wish for the love of a person they are attracted to, and when they receive it, they end up in a miserable and destructive relationship. Just because their intention was not to love back. Instead, it was to substitute a black spot on their framed painting."

"Did those people cut your trees?"

"Yes. They thought we had fooled them. Men, women, even children came with saws and axes and hacked down one tree after another. Both the enchanted and the ordinary. We couldn't have done anything. Crazed with anger, they killed my mom, my dad, and my little sister too. I survived only because I had been hiding inside that big stump.

"When they eventually realized what they had done, looking at the dead bodies and the blood on their hands, they panicked, ran away, and haven't returned since.

"From that day, I have been looking after what is left. It's my destiny. I can't imagine any better life."

"Don't you miss your family?"

"I do. But, in a way, they are always here with me," the woman said and stroked the boulders they were sitting on.

"You say people shouldn't eat fruit from the wish trees. But this orchard is here for a reason, right? If it was your family who had planted those trees, you must know the whole story."

"My dad would tell me only what he had heard from his dad. And that is that the granddad of his granddad planted the first tree of this kind."

The trees, the grass, the wind, as well as the sun fell silent and pricked up their ears.

"Jacob was born to a poor family. He had exactly three sisters and three brothers. All six were blond, only Jacob's head was crowned in brown unruly curls.

"Their parents were struggling to provide food for the whole lot of them. Sometimes, when the siblings were too hungry, their dad would tell fabulous stories at night to make it easier for them to fall asleep.

"One of those stories spoke about a princess who was bedridden with an odd illness that made it painful for her to walk, or even raise her arms to feed herself. She refused to talk to anyone and spent her days staring out of the windows in her cheerless chamber."

The castle is surrounded by the most exquisite garden the Earth has ever seen. Yet, she doesn't find any joy in looking at the exotic plants and lovely flowers. The only thing she dreams about is for the trees to bear fruit that would fulfill any of her wishes. She likes to imagine wearing dresses so breathtaking and jewelry so dazzling that all the noblewomen from far and near would be jealous of her.

Her dad, the king, is sad for his daughter to be suffering that much. Once, he has it announced that a man who can plant such a tree in the royal garden will be rewarded with one coffer of sparkling emeralds, one coffer of indigo sapphires, and one coffer of black pearls.

Despite the promise of a great fortune, people all around the kingdom, both rich and poor, believe that the request of their king is utter nonsense.

For many months, the king and his queen are waiting for someone to appear at the court with a magical seed, but to no avail.

Until one day, a well-dressed man, riding a silver Arabian stallion, arrives at their gates. And he demands to be granted an audience with the princess herself. Since his dress suggests that he may be a prince from the Far Orient, the king reluctantly agrees.

The man enters the dark chamber and kneels down, facing the princess. He reaches into his pocket and pulls out a folded silk handkerchief.

Then he extends his hand.

The princess lazily lifts her eyes and parts her lips as if she wants to say a word, but nothing comes out. The man unfolds the handkerchief and reveals a small amber seed. He tells the princess that the seed will grow into a tree and this tree will bear fruit that can make any of her wishes come true. He also tells her that she needs to plant the seed herself, water its roots every day, and watch it grow.

The king is appalled, the queen laughs nervously, only the princess feels something snug and pulsing around her heart, and after several long minutes almost imperceptibly blinks her eyes in consent.

The next day, they bring her to the garden in a wheeled chair. With the help of the foreigner, she plants the seed into the ground, and for the first time in years, she breathes fresh air and feels the warmth of the sun on her pale face.

It doesn't take long before she needs no support. She leaves her room every morning on her own feet to water the seedlings and other plants in the garden. She spends long hours with the stranger who tells her about traditions and beauties of his homeland.

Years pass.

Our princess turns into a healthy woman with strong legs, strong arms, and a very strong heart. She and the foreign prince get married, and when the tree bears its first fruit, the princess cuts it into two equal halves and shares it with her husband. They both wish for their love to give birth to a baby boy.

When the child is born, the man takes his wife, their son, and three full coffers away to his faraway land.

The princess never sees her parents again since they die of grief soon after. The land is without a ruler for a long time, the castle wastes away, its garden is seized by weed and shadow, and everyone forgets the tree that, once a year, bears magical fruit.

While the woman spoke, the darkness broken by a soft stellar glow covered the sky above their heads.

"Since Jacob heard this bedtime story, he wouldn't stop thinking about the tree. He put his mind to finding it and bringing its fruit to his brothers and sisters.

"Of course, he knew that it would not be clever to eat it all at once. He would keep its seeds to grow some of his own!

"Because they were poor, they had never received any presents for their birthdays, like children from wealthy families do. He figured that once the tree started bearing, they would wish every year for a toy to share among them.

"Jacob was too little back then to think about entering adulthood one day. He just wanted to play.

"His parents couldn't afford to send their children to school, so Jacob had to look elsewhere if he were to learn about growing trees. Especially the magical ones.

"One day, he sneaked out of their home and went to see a woman whom the whole village called 'the witch.'

"She was in her early thirties, a beautiful tall brunette with foxy eyes. Although he had once overheard his dad telling his mom that the woman deserved to be tied up naked and lashed as a dog, Jacob was not scared.

"The woman invited Jacob to her house and gave him a cup of cold hibiscus tea.

"The boy told her what he was looking for.

"She didn't laugh at him as he had expected. She sat quietly, listening to him, her long ominous fingers softly tapping the wooden table to the rhythm of his heartbeat.

"Jacob asked her if she had ever heard about the castle with the most wonderful garden the Earth had ever seen and its magical tree.

"The woman had no reason to lie to him. She had never heard about such a tree. The story was a mere fairy tale, to make hungry children fall asleep.

"She asked about his dad though. Was it him who came up with the story? How was he doing? Did he know that Jacob had gone to her house?

"The boy told her that his dad would barely reply to his many questions, and if he pushed too much, he would risk getting beaten. He was not sure how to respond to her second question, but he assured her that his parents had no idea that he went to see her.

"She apologized that she could not help him find the tree. She offered instead that she would teach him everything she knew about wild herbs and remedial plants.

"The woman was sick and, many a day, her body left her hurting and tired. Despite her young age, she felt she was going to pass away soon. She knew how to heal various injuries and diseases, but she failed to heal herself of the wound deepest, her broken heart.

"The tender luster of Jacob's eyes promised hope that the treasure of her knowledge wouldn't be squandered.

"Over the following months, she taught him everything she had learned from her own mother.

"He was a fast learner. The only thing he did not learn was how to grow a tree whose fruit would turn a wish into a long-dreamt-of toy.

"The day the woman decided to leave this world, she made him remember three things.

"Firstly, she asked him to always treat his new skills as a great gift of life. She said he was not bound to pursue any particular vocation. However, whatever he did, he should always strive to improve himself, learn, and aim at the very best in his profession of choice.

"Secondly, she told him to remember that to heal a broken heart and a wounded spirit is more difficult than to heal a wounded body. She advised him to always look into people's eyes, inspect steadiness of their breath, and check the strength of their handshake. She said that life taught her that many bodily ailments, in fact, proceeded from a corrupted character, disturbed mind, or shattered self-esteem.

"Lastly, she made him promise that he would keep looking for value in things and people, regardless of their looks, words, and actions. She told him that every thing and every person has been brought to this world for some reason, and sometimes they just need a bit of help and a push in the right direction.

"When the final sigh left her sorrowful body, Jacob had returned to his parents.

"He had never revealed the truth of his visits to the forbidden lady to them. His mom had seldom shown interest in his matters anyway, and his dad was a charismatic man, a great storyteller, yet quite fearsome at times, so he simply decided to avoid them both as much as possible.

"As he grew up, people started noticing his flair for plants and herbs. Occasionally, they would ask him to prepare a relaxing tea or an ointment for aching knees.

"Jacob was one of them, a kind and fine-looking boy. They had soon learned to respect him for what his teacher was loathed and rejected for.

"When he turned into a full grown-up, he became a highly regarded healer and herbalist. People from all over the country came to meet him, and they also paid fairly good money for his advice and medicine.

"Jacob was a happy man. He could afford to build a house for his wife and their first child, which she was just carrying. He was helping people by doing what he loved. His brothers and sisters loved him and after their parents died, they unconditionally supported each other.

"Only one thing was missing. Jacob had not forgotten his dream. The dream about a tree that bears wish-fulfilling fruit.

"He had never shared this dream with anyone except for his wife, for he knew people don't forgive if you dare to dream beyond the limits of their imagination.

"When he met her for the first time, he was so charmed that he forgot to be careful and told her everything about his passion for plants. He also told her the story of a melancholic princess and a foreigner on a silver Arabian horse.

"After he finished, he looked into her eyes and held her trustful hands in his. And he knew she understood. An aureole of potent energy was born to surround them forever, no matter if they were close or thousands of miles apart, no matter if one of them died or left for another, this energy was independent of their will, and even more powerful for both of them contributed to its inception alike.

"When they became old, Jacob asked his wife for permission to set off on a long journey. He didn't want to die without at least making an attempt to look for the wish tree beyond the borders of their land. By then, they had saved up enough means to support all their children and their new families, so he didn't need to work any extra days simply for the sake of making money.

"His wife agreed on one condition: that he would do his best to come back in one piece. Then she revealed to him her long-kept secret too. When she herself was a little girl, she also had a dream. A dream in her sleep, about a boy with a crown of unruly curls. When Jacob came to her life, she didn't ask anything else from life. Nevertheless, she received more than she could have ever hoped for.

"Jacob once again took her creased hands into his and gave her his word that they would pass the last days of their lives together. He closed his practice, and packed a few selected ointments, potions, and herbal blends into his sack. Even though he had plenty of golden coins on him, he knew that in certain situations the value of money is negligible, while the value of a helping hand may prove critical.

"On his travels, he learned about many new plants and new herbs. He also developed new potions, new medicines, and new balms, which he offered to people to express his thanks for their hospitality.

"Soon, the word spread about his kindness and generosity, and he was invited to stay here and there. Often, he didn't have to pay for his food, or even for a bed to put his head down.

"Everywhere he set his foot, he talked to people, old and young, and listened to their stories and fairy tales. He also shared his own, those he would tell to his children when they were still little and unsuspecting. And when they asked for more, he told them a story of a castle with the most beautiful garden the Earth had ever seen.

"He was hoping that one day, someone, somewhere, would reveal that he had heard a similar history. He was looking for any clue to prove to himself that the old story was not a mere fantasy of his childish soul. He wanted to believe that if something makes a dent in your heart you are not able to mend, then it stays there for a reason.

"One day, he reached a flat country with hot climate and tall snow-capped mountains on the edge of an endless horizon. The first people he met and asked for accommodation brought him to a house which looked like a dull fortress with an iron gate on the outside, but in reality harbored a splendid palace that welcomed him with a refreshing blow of cold breeze.

"The owner of the hotel had his housemaid prepare a spacious room for him by the very rooftop. This suited Jacob well since it had become his favorite pastime to sit in silence and clear his head by observing other people.

"Just to stay still for a few long minutes and watch people talk to each other, laugh, move things around…

"That way, he would often learn more about them and mankind as such than during all those years when he was

busy tending to dozens of his patients. Rather than getting carried away by the occasional sting of homesickness,
he would take his chair out on the balcony and simply look
down below him.

"One day, he caught sight of a shy woman who was nervously pacing across the teal mosaic on the ground floor.
After a while, she seated herself on a sofa by the wall and
kept staring mindlessly into a fountain in the middle of the
courtyard. Then, she opened her bag and pulled out a large
embroidered handkerchief to wipe her squarish face, which
seemed to be sweating, even though the temperature inside
the old house was more than pleasant.

"She must have been thirsty, but she didn't ask the housemaid for a cup of water, nor did she approach the fountain to
cool down her clenched palms.

"Jacob saw a woman who had a heavy burden to carry, yet
she was not used to asking for help. She took pride in accepting whatever life offered her without a hint of bitterness,
without a desire for change.

"When she got up and was about to leave, Jacob realized
that the woman had not only been waiting for someone; she
was waiting for that little push people sometimes need to
start flapping their wings.

"So he descended the stairs to open the little door of her
birdcage.

"The woman's cheeks blushed with a combination of
unease and expectation when he greeted her a good day.
She instantly knew who he was. There had been talk about
a healer who had come to town from far away and who saw
right through people's souls.

"She didn't particularly want someone to peer into her
soul. This was a far too abstract concept for her to grasp, and

she didn't appreciate any of its value. On the other hand, she was a practical woman with quite a practical problem.

"When they sat down, she introduced herself as Camelia. Jacob's face lit up with a wide smile instantly.

"What a wonderful name! He asked her if she knew its origin.

"She replied that her mother liked the idea of calling her daughter after a flower. Her eyes looked down as if she was ashamed of something quite so foolish.

"Jacob explained to her, with unparalleled enthusiasm in his voice, that camellias are beneficial flowers whose petals please one's eye, whose smell pleases one's nose, whose seeds give oil that prevents skin from aging, and whose leaves make delicious tea!

"The woman seemed undecided whether to become confused or flattered. Nevertheless, Jacob earned her trust with his candid interest, so she plucked up courage to open her heart to him.

"She told him that the real reason she had hoped to meet him was her early pregnancy. The family of her husband was haunted by a mysterious curse, which caused all the babies delivered to be boys. Not a single girl had been born as far as any one of them could remember.

"Camelia was expecting her first, and even though she was certain she would love her child no matter if it was a girl or a boy, she wished from the bottom of her heart to give birth to a daughter.

"'Girls make for better helpers in the household,' she explained.

"'And better friends!' Jacob added.

"It was obvious to him that the woman sitting across from him was lonely. There was a huge heart beating vigorously in her proud chest. It was overflowing with love that she had no one to share with.

"Jacob was sorry for not being able to help her. He apologized to Camelia for his skill was limited. He hadn't the slightest idea how to break the curse so she could bring a baby girl into her family. Nonetheless, he offered her an herbal blend, which would alleviate the stiffness and pain in her lower back and reduce morning sickness. He also promised her that once he found camellia flowers on his travels, he would prepare special oil for her skin and her raven hair. And he would make sure to send it to her no matter where in the world he was.

"The young woman was not disappointed. She had done her best, and she was at peace. Besides, she had met a new friend who made her feel somehow special.

"Since she didn't yet want to lose him as fast, she insisted that he come to their house for a family dinner.

"Jacob gladly accepted.

"The following day, they sent a carriage, which brought him to a house that was even more uninviting on the outside and even more comfortable on the inside than the hotel he was staying at.

"Camelia introduced him to her husband and to many of her brothers-in-law. The women of the household stayed in the kitchen, preparing an array of delicious courses, laughing, sipping coffee, and gossiping about their men. Their chattering resonated in the hallway like a cascade of coins jumping down the stairs.

"As they walked through the main salon, Jacob noticed a remarkable painting of a silver Arabian stallion hanging on the wall. The horse carried an elegant man together with no less than three leather coffers.

"Jacob's heart almost leaped out of his chest. He instantly forgot about the dinner, about anything that was happening around. In that very moment, the Earth stopped revolving, the stars dimmed their light out of courtesy, and it was just him.

"And the art piece on the wall.

"When Camelia saw that Jacob froze on the spot as if hypnotized, she told him that the man in the frame was a great-great-granddad of her husband. She also revealed that there had been a legend running in her family of the coffers being hidden somewhere in the garden at the back of the house. In the past, various members of the family had turned the ground upside down in vain. But they had never found anything so they had eventually given up.

"'Obviously!' she sneered.

"She took him by his arm and gently brought him outside to catch some fresh air.

"The garden gave the impression that it had been neglected for quite some time. Camelia explained that the only tree that had ever grown there was one twisted lemon tree, which gave deformed fruit and whose juice offered an unpleasant vinegary taste. But although its lemons were barely edible and gave a person an awful stomachache, the family had never cut it down. Somehow they felt it was an integral part of their home and its history. Except for that, her dear guest could at most take delight in the abundance of wild flowers that had overtaken every inch of the place.

"Jacob softly leaned on Camelia with his fragile body.

"An old man. A man who had lived a good life.

"A lot was fleeting through his mind at that moment. However, unlike young people who squander their time on getting caught in the spiderweb of their thoughts, he was patiently waiting for the right one.

"Just when a wee feathery dandelion parachute landed on his arched nose, he remembered the last words of his mother.

"Even an outcast tree bearing sour fruit could provide for a disguised value!

"He asked Camelia for permission to take one crinkled lemon home with him. When she wondered why, he didn't lie. He said he believed it might fulfill one of his wishes.

"For the first time in months, Camelia wholeheartedly laughed. Her new friend was truly an eccentric fellow. She liked him a lot.

"After a long dinner, where each of the twelve courses was tastier than the previous one, Jacob returned to his room, exhausted, with the lemon in his left pocket. He slept for twelve long hours, wrapped in deep, satisfied sleep.

"The next day, he began his journey home. This time he didn't stop, because he couldn't wait to reunite with the love of his life, who was waiting every single day for him to come back. Only once did he spend three days in a village that boasted a vast field of camellias.

"One landowner sold him an armful. He could have offered the flowers for free since, for him, they were nothing but a bothersome weed. But Jacob was a foreigner. The tradition commanded to rip off the gentleman at least a tiny bit.

"Jacob then found a mayor, who also operated a pressing machine, and had him make oil of the camellia seeds. The good man wished to help Jacob for no charge, but the machine had not been in use for quite some time, and he was hoping to bring home a few coins. Even so, he was genuinely surprised that Jacob paid more than fair price just for filling one tiny flask.

"Jacob countered, saying that there was never too little. It's the small things, not big gestures, which make true friends.

"Then he sold his last herbal teas to reward the third man, a painter who was traveling far away towards the East to find his muse. He believed that upon meeting such a woman, he would be inspired to make a portrait to be admired by generations, long after his own death.

"They found soulmates in each other, and the artist didn't accept any money for Jacob's request. He cheerfully agreed to pass by the town of the woman with raven hair. Much like Jacob himself, he believed that if life gives you a chance to explore something unexpected, you should take it without asking twice.

"Without any unnecessary words, they hugged, wished good luck to one another, and parted their ways. Jacob was certain that one bright day the painter would succeed in meeting his muse, and by her side would greet his destiny. He seemed to be one of those few rare people who emanate energy that sometimes drives a man to do feats on the brink of craziness. Jacob was of the opinion that one should always surround themselves with people of such kind, because their energy is predominantly positive, if you harness it for a good cause, and moreover: contagious. The more you get hold of it, the more you can achieve anything your imagination can think of.

"The herbalist's odyssey was approaching its end.

"In a couple of weeks, he reached home and at last reunited with his family. With great pride, he showed his wife the ugly, sour lemon fruit, and told her about everything he had experienced and about all the people he had met.

"Jacob's wife was happy. And she was certainly not jealous. Her husband was back home, a bit older, and significantly poorer, but with a pocket full of stories that would fill their evenings for many years to come. Even though she couldn't keep him company on his travels, she was at least offered no less than the fine privilege of watching the whole journey being relayed in the reflection of his radiant eyes.

"The separation made their marriage even stronger. They didn't ask life for anything more than to spend their last years together.

"Jacob had made his dream come true. He had found a tree that bore wish-fulfilling fruit. And what's more, he had seen a majestic painting of a man riding his silver horse. The man who had cured and kidnapped a melancholic princess.

"Despite his high age, he felt as if once again he was a little boy living in one of his dad's fabulous stories. The boy for whom nothing was impossible and everything was within reach of his little soft hands.

"Since his homecoming, Jacob had spent many hours describing the painting to his wife, because he wanted to share with her that one moment when the world stopped, and Jacob understood that his spirit didn't lie.

"Together, they planted seeds of the fruit Jacob had brought back home with him.

"For the stones were everything they needed, they threw away the rest, which was eaten by a stray dog. If it had secretly wished for something, we will never know.

"They also planted many other trees to bear fruits of different shapes, colors, and tastes. The orchard was a present to their children, partly to serve as an eternal memory, partly as a commitment to explore their own desires and hopes.

The old couple believed that everyone, including their only son and their only daughter, ought to deserve their dreams first, just like Jacob did when he traveled across many lands to find his tree, and as did his wife when she patiently waited for the love of her life.

"When they finished sowing the seeds and building a fence around the orchard to be, they called the children and asked them to take good care of the trees after their death. They told them that some day one of them might bear a fruit that would make their wishes come true. They also said that it was important to learn which fruits to enjoy and which to keep for the right time. And that they should not reveal its secret to people who were not ready to fight for what they really wanted.

"Jacob and his wife had seen the little trees grow, yet they had not lived long enough to taste any of what they would give.

"Jacob had indeed nothing to regret. He had cured many people. He had visited exotic countries. He had been learning and discovering new things until the last moments of his daring life. He had taken the risk and bet his fortune on finding one ugly, sour lemon, which he had cut and put back to the ground. He had founded an orchard of trees that would bring fruit for generations to come and taught his children how to recognize what was worth fighting for.

"Jacob and his wife passed peacefully in their sleep. As every night, they held each other's hand, so Estelle could finally accompany her husband on one more glorious expedition, this time towards the mighty stars.

"The young man and woman followed the advice of their beloved parents to keep the legacy of the orchard alive. But the inevitable was inevitable, and Florian eventually decided to leave his sister to seek the treasure their father had told them about just before he left them for good. The coffers full of precious stones and the garden, which in its endless patience was waiting to be devastated one more time, kept disturbing his uneasy mind.

"Tessla, on the other hand, stayed home and waited for the lemon tree to bloom and give its first fruit. She had never had any doubts about what Papa had shared with her. However, after all the work she had put into maintaining the garden, she felt entitled to be the first one to give the wish tree a try.

"Once the third spring arrived, a small crinkled fruit appeared on the highest branch. Even uglier than the one Jacob had brought home many years ago.

"When she climbed the tree to pick the lemon, she slipped and fell down. She broke her leg, which soon turned out to have crippled her forever, but as luck would have it, the fruit stayed in her hand.

"She bit into the sour flesh and wished for a friend to break her loneliness. With her brother gone, it was hard to pass through long days without anybody to talk to.

"The next day, when she was lying in bed and recovering from her injury, a bird appeared in the garden. It was not the friend she had imagined, but it was so beautiful that it made her look forward to every new day just to peek through the window and watch him repose in the crown of the magic lemon tree.

"Her dad made her a keeper of a secret, and secrets make your heart heavier than usual. What's more, the orchard asked for a lot of hard work, and due to her brand new incapacity to move around as before, she needed to look for a pair of helping hands.

"When she was able to limp out of the house and approach the bird, she tried to tell him everything she knew about the orchard and other plants in her dad's garden. Even though the bird didn't respond, her heart was relieved.

"The following morning, she had it announced that she was looking for a strong worker who would not mind spending most of his waking hours among an awful lot of trees. The next day, a man arrived at her bed. Somewhat oddly, and to her big surprise, he kneeled down to offer his service.

"She never saw the bird again."

The child's eyes were narrow with tiredness, but she kept listening until the very end. She didn't dare to interrupt the old woman, whose own eyelids were falling down a tad with every word. When she finished her story, a crisp morning had already replaced the tranquil night.

When the last word was spoken, as if in unison, they both laid their heads down and fell asleep without wishing good night to each other. Their bodies fatigued as if they had just lived the whole lifetime of Jacob themselves—planting, watering, and watching his trees grow.

When they woke up later in the afternoon, the child proposed to the woman to stay with her. It was just the right time to make things right.

She asked her to teach her everything. The child would be her arms and legs, and together they would save the very little that had been spared many years ago.

Sagitta was glad to have the child keep her company, so she agreed without much hesitation. She gave her the tools she had been keeping in the tree stump to remember her mom and dad and her slaughtered sibling by.

The girl worked dawn to dusk for many weeks to make the orchard look more like an actual garden and less like an enchanted forest. Since they both needed to eat something other than the fruit, she collected it every morning and sold it to people in the surrounding villages. She also found a childless couple who was willing to move into the abandoned dwelling that was adjoining the orchard on the north end and oversee it in exchange for a part of the sale proceeds.

There was nothing to fear. By then, the villagers had already forgotten what their ancestors, once upon a time, had done to one quirky family. The story of the fruit that can fulfill any wish had become a fairy tale once again.

Time passed rather faster than slower.

One day, the girl woke up and recognized the familiar feeling which makes a person take a few steps forward. She said goodbye to the woman who taught her one has to be cautious about what she or he really wants. Because when we really want something, there's a high chance that it happens, and then we have to eat what we have cooked for ourselves.

They hugged, and Sagitta gave her five kisses on each cheek to protect her from the evil. She told her:

"Remember, my little lady, that Life is generous. Don't expect anything from him but always ask for a lot. If you don't ask, he will eventually turn his back on you."

Then, with a glimmer of tears in her eyes, she handed her a basket of the finest fruits the orchard would offer, including one sour lemon.

"Appreciate what you have and don't grieve for what you haven't got. Focus on what you can do, not what you are unable to do. Pay attention to what's happening now, not what happened in the past or what may happen in the future. Move forward but stay still."

Without saying anything else, she began silently walking to her home in the giant mossy stump. After a while, she turned back one last time and murmured:

"But what do I know. I'm just an old woman who likes to talk."

The child shouted back:

"Oh no. You're a queen. A queen of an enchanted orchard!"

Sagitta giggled and replied:

"Maybe. Maybe I'm a queen. I guess it's just a matter of perspective..." Then she disappeared from the child's sight for good.

After a week of walking, the child reached home. All the fruits she had received from the old woman were long gone, except for the lemon, which she kept in her back pocket.

The place had changed.

She found herself facing a row of short buildings, connected by a paved road, and surrounded by many blooming trees. The villagers greeted her as if they had always known her, as if she had never left her hut.

She looked around to find her bird. And once again she felt a swelling pressure under her rib cage. Her soul told her that she would never see the old friend again because they had already soared above the clouds, forever, together.

When she looked up, she finally realized that her home had changed because she had changed herself.

She pulled the lemon out of her pocket.

She could have wished for anything she had ever wanted. But... her journey had barely begun. She had still so much to learn and so much to paint. It was not time yet.

She threw the fruit to the children, who were standing by the road, to play with. It was unlikely that they would bite into an ugly sour fruit.

Yet, who knows?

Children explore the world around them with their senses. They smell, touch, and taste to learn. They take a chance on things that adults find uninteresting, or even repulsive. That's why the fabulous canvases of their minds don't have any boundaries. That's why their dreams are born out of joy and determination.

The hut was gone. Instead, she arrived at a house that was guarded by a proud, green-eyed, silky cat on the roof. She pushed the door with the hands of a child, and entered as a woman. She was not alone.

18. What You Do vs. Who You Are

Traditionally, when we talk about BUSINESS, one of the first free associations that would come to our minds is MONEY. In the recent years, though, ENTREPRENEURSHIP has been gaining in popularity together with the rise of technology, while being tightly associated with the concept of INNOVATION.

When we talk about innovation, it's a common misconception to think solely of computers, gadgets, laboratories, or hefty research grants. INNOVATION MEANS DESIGNING A BETTER SOLUTION FOR AN EXISTING NEED WITH THE GOAL OF BRINGING POSITIVE CHANGE TO PEOPLE'S LIVES. It happens all around the world at various scales, starting from very small local communities.

For modern entrepreneurs, innovation goes both ways. They develop solutions, products, or services that address needs of their customers better than any of the available substitutes. At the same time, they use the latest outputs of innovation and new technologies to improve their productivity, save their costs, facilitate communication, and foster collaboration.

Every individual can innovate, regardless of where they live and what resources are at their disposal. Every individual, even without having acquired formal education or training, possesses a unique skillset and formative experience. And every individual who is driven to deliver improved solutions, or come up with original ones, is usually also driven to continually work on developing new skills so that they succeed in their mission in the best way possible.

> **Running a business is about what you do, while being an entrepreneur is about who you are.**

The purpose of launching and owning a business is to generate profit by meeting the customer demand with the supply of your products or services at a given price and quantity. In the absence of profit, there's obviously little reason for the existence of a for-profit company.

Entrepreneurs, on the other hand, are individuals whose set of beliefs and principles moves them to build businesses with the objective of improving lives of other people, including their own.

Money is not their primary motivation, yet they are certainly NOT ALTRUISTS.

They are on the lookout for business opportunities that solve REAL EXISTING PROBLEMS.

They strive to contribute to their communities, while at the same time generating FINANCIAL RETURNS, on a scale that justifies sustainable profitability.

They surround themselves with like-minded individuals who share their mission and vision, and leverage the POTENTIAL OF COLLABORATION.

> Entrepreneurs are innovators who build sustainable businesses or engage in projects that make a real positive impact.

Sustainable businesses maximize positive impact on society and minimize negative impact on the environment while generating revenue that warrants creation of jobs and further investment into its activities. Sometimes to build such a business, entrepreneurs need to invest a substantial amount of their own capital and give up personal income for an extended period of time. They will experiment on a daily basis and most probably fail more than once.

Luckily, for a true entrepreneur, not a single failure means a step backward, but rather a jump forward. Without failure, they would never learn and see things as they really are, rather than as they wish them to be.

Nevertheless, it doesn't mean that entrepreneurs don't have their downs, where doubts and fear may blur their good judgment. In such moments, they simply need to keep going, keep improving, while holding on to the belief that their purpose in life is to create lasting value of some kind.

It takes a brave and resilient individual to give up short-term growth and profit for the sake of long-term social innovation. There are many brilliant businessmen and businesswomen among us who contribute to local and global economies, but much fewer entrepreneurs. To become one is a lifelong commitment, and it's definitely not for everybody.

19. As You Sow, so Shall You Reap

Entrepreneurs undertake CREATIVE AND ECONOMIC ACTIVITIES and assume the risk of INVESTING THEIR OWN AND ACQUIRED RESOURCES, with the objective of increasing the accrued value of both, which habitually means making a profit.

However, if we look at all the resources invested by an individual, one at a time, we can see that MONETARY PROFIT IS NOT THE SOLE EXPRESSION OF THE EARNED VALUE. When we dare to look beyond the quantifiable and tangible, we realize that our perception of failure or success in business might have been somehow flat.

> Numbers don't always tell the right story.

One minus on paper can live next to thousands of pluses in reality, tied to certain moments or incremental improvements in other people's lives and our own. If we choose to acknowledge their significance, we attain the most priceless gift of all: FREEDOM. Numbers become but practical tools, not relentless slave masters. Time turns from a mortal enemy into our good friend. Money appears to be a welcome benefit, not an eagerly anticipated goal in itself.

To understand the complete value entrepreneurs can create and gain, we need to go much deeper when considering all the resources they invest on their personal level. These include:

TIME

Time is an absolutely limited and non-retrievable resource.

In simple terms, it means that at a point A we are born and at a point B we die. Naturally, the more we move along away from A, the closer we get to B. We just never know how close we are.

The good news is that it's in our power to make the line segment between A and B somewhat longer. And that is not only by maintaining a healthy lifestyle but also by SPENDING OUR TIME IN A WAY THAT WE FIND OURSELVES WHERE WE WANT TO BE at any given moment.

Sometimes a year passes and we find it hard to believe how fast our life has been racing forward. Sometimes we look back and marvel at the multitude of things we have experienced in a small amount of time.

Not accomplished; experienced.

To experience means to live. To live means to feel, to laugh or to cry, to love and to be loved. To live means to spend your days doing not what you should be doing or what you are expected to be doing, but what you want to be doing.

When we talk about time being limited, the problem in question is not only our own productivity and the jaded mantra "work smart, not hard." Time is obviously limited regardless of our working habits, occupation, or life goals.

TO LIVE MEANS TO SPEND YOUR DAYS DOING NOT WHAT YOU SHOULD BE DOING...
...OR WHAT YOU ARE EXPECTED TO BE DOING...
...BUT WHAT YOU WANT TO BE DOING.

It's not about how many hours we work and how many hours we rest. It's not about doing as much work as possible in as little time as possible. It's about turning the time passed into something that lasts, not always in its physical form, but at least in thoughts, memories, and hearts.

Most entrepreneurs assume that the principal questions that stand before them are: "Do I have sufficient capital to do this? Am I good enough? Am I strong enough? Do I know the right people? What if I fail and lose everything? How do I reduce the risks to the minimum and achieve something substantial?"

Yet, the real question stands:

"Am I going to use my finite time allowance in the absolutely best way possible?"

Business is often quite tough enough. One may lose money or property, one may break important relationships, and one may have their self-esteem crushed. At the same time, there's always a chance that one can earn new money after that, build new relationships, and raise the self-esteem from the ashes.

But time is different. You have only one chance to make every minute count. If you manage to do that, there's no such thing as failure.

THE VALUE CREATED LIES IN THE TIME SPENT DOING SOMETHING THAT WAS WORTH YOUR WHILE.

Entrepreneurs shall be prudent and rational about administering their finances. However, if they suck with numbers, it's still less of a catastrophe than if they suck at handling their time.

Unlike time, which simply is out there for us to use it or lose it, energy needs to be created or actively searched for. Besides, one can always make or find more, and there are quite a few ways to do so.

Every challenging journey, be it chasing dreams or solving problems big and small, should then begin with an energy diet, locating hidden energy reserves, and plugging leaking energy loopholes.

To use an analogy, being on a diet doesn't usually mean to stop eating. It means regulating the quantities we consume and picking food of higher quality and nutritional value. The first step would then be to ditch junk food, i.e., food that makes you full but is not beneficial to your body.

In similar fashion, being on an energy diet doesn't mean to stay passive. It means reducing the amount of energy we spend on things that bring little value. The first step would then be to DITCH JUNK ACTIVITIES, i.e., activities that make you feel occupied and engaged, yet except for consuming this scarce resource of yours, they don't offer any beneficial contribution to your life or your work.

Without energy, we don't exist, we can't advance anywhere.

A thought requires a certain amount of energy to exist and evolve into an idea. An emotion needs energy to transform into action.

Therefore, not only your body but above all your mind and your spirit need a hell of a lot of energy to serve you well.

The crucial and inevitable measure to enhance your energy level is to take good care of your BODY. It's not that complicated since all you need to do is to pay attention to these five basic activities: *breathing, sleeping, eating, drinking,* and *exercising.*

As obvious as they may seem, this is where people lose most of their energy. At the same time, they are fairly easy to fix. A proper breathing technique, a few extra hours of good-quality sleep, healthier eating habits, an occasional walk or moderate workout, and regular hydration usually result in giant leaps towards a balanced mindset, improved physical fitness, and greater productivity.

When your THOUGHTS and EMOTIONS seem to be out of control, you can meditate as much as you want, do countless power poses, or recite heaps of motivational platitudes, and none of that will help if your body is not working as it should be.

Our emotions are simply reactions of our body, which in turn are affected by our thoughts. A strong body is able to control its mind by selecting which thoughts and feelings to accept and which to ignore.

Next, you can move onto preserving energy by maintaining healthy RELATIONSHIPS.

Your interactions with other people basically fall into two categories: those who leave you charged with extra energy and those who leave you drained.

Often it's the person themselves who acts either as an energy-giver or an energy-sucker; sometimes it's us who create an experience of communicating with a particular person in a way that it leaves us emotionally or physically exhausted.

When our energy bars are empty, the immunity system of our mind is weak and automatically switches from a creator to a victim mode. Instead of having full control over our experience, we are left at the mercy of external stimuli.

There is a perfect term for these phenomena: "taking things personally." What people say and how they act is suddenly all about us.

> He is so rude "to me." She doesn't understand "my" needs. They have just humiliated "me." No one appreciates "me." They only care about themselves, and "I'm" so lonely. I need to do everything "myself" because everyone else is useless. It's "me" against them...

Relationships with other people have an immense impact on both our physical and mental strength. It's not uncommon for a person to develop a chronic disease because they have been stuck in an unhealthy relationship, or for a person to feel unwell because of a toxic work environment.

The more important role a person plays in your life, the more any dysfunction between you and them either destroys or empowers you, be it your life or your business partner, for instance.

In conclusion, the art of preserving, making, and storing adequate amounts of energy to create, build, and lead is a vital skill for any successful entrepreneur.

Human Capital

Entrepreneurs further invest their unique combination of personal characteristics, knowledge, skills, experience, and creativity. This resource is not only expandable but also shareable.

The more you put in and the more you share with others, the more you gain back.

It rarely happens for a person to be less skilled or experienced at the end of their entrepreneurial journey. When they feel as if they had lost motivation or even sense of creativity, it's most probably just an emotion associated with hurt self-esteem, which can be healed, or a critically low level of energy, which can be duly re-created.

All in all, your knowledge and skills naturally flourish and deepen with every step taken, task accomplished, project developed, or enterprise launched, therefore, on an individual level, the value generated is self-evident.

Entrepreneurship is a special, demanding school. Sometimes it's costly, and sometimes it takes an eternity to finish. And on top of that, you don't even get a shining diploma.

But what you do get is a first-class education in problem solving, leadership, team building, communication, networking, project management, sales, marketing, budgeting, fund-raising... and, most of all, resiliency. Not that bad at all.

SOCIAL CAPITAL

We don't live in a vacuum, and thus the prospect of us being successful largely depends on our ability to reap the benefits of our social connections and to foster meaningful relationships with other people. Our personal network is a resource that takes long years to build and is held together by several, rather fragile, components:

TRUST

We hear successful businessmen say, "I don't trust any-body," or "Trust, but verify." However, without a bare minimum of trust present, no economic activity—such as the exchange of goods, services, or money—could exist.

When my actions involve expectations about your future behavior (e.g., I will provide you with something and you will pay me back), I believe in your intentions and ability to deliver a certain outcome or make things I care about happen.

RECIPROCITY

For a relationship to enter into our disposable social capital, it needs to embody the mutual exchange of benefits.

You do help people, and one day, they may help you in return. You treat them with respect, and you earn respect. You provide value to others, and you receive some value yourself.

The parties of any human interaction have their own distinct interests to follow. What makes a meaningful relationship stand out is when you not only ask yourself, "What's in it for me?" but also, "What can I give?"

COLLABORATION

When two or more people share the same goal and their skills, which are vital for such a goal to come to fruition, are complementary, we may witness the sheer power of collaboration.

You and I are not a mere sum of our individual knowledge, expertise, and abilities. By working together, we multiply the outcome of our efforts. We support each other because when either of us wins, we both become winners.

VALUES

Shared values are a mother to successful collaboration, reciprocity, and trust.

Sharing the same goal and sharing the same values are not the same things. A goal is something you aim to achieve within a defined timeframe. A value is something that originates from your core beliefs.

If you meet your goals, you will attain a certain level of satisfaction, which may or may not last. If your goals and actions are aligned with your values, you experience deep gratification, joy, and harmony.

PURPOSE

People can be part of your social network even if your interests and motivations differ.

However, if you aim to leverage your personal connections for building a successful and sustainable business, it helps when those who provide you with support and resources along the way have faith in the same purpose. This inevitably reflects on the quality of communication and engagement of all the invested parties.

When your partners and coworkers share a common purpose, moments of uncertainty and conflict are much easier to get through.

IDENTITY

Our personal network is an essential factor in sculpting our own identity.

People we meet and surround ourselves with have an immense impact on our potential to reach success. We're influenced by their beliefs, by their ambitions, by their ability to deal with adversity. Their flawed self-esteem can drag us down; their deficient reserves of energy can cause them to deplete our own.

On the contrary, people who believe in themselves tend to believe in others as well. Their positive attitudes are highly contagious and empowering. In their eyes, their success is sealed by the prosperity of other people, including you.

In essence, our social capital is our safety net which prevents us from falling and which supports us when we grow. Its fibers become stronger and more resilient with every bit of value we create and share with each other.

FACTORS OF PRODUCTION

The classic inputs that are necessary for the production of goods and services are as follows:

LAND – all natural resources and energy sources

CAPITAL – own or borrowed (money, cars, buildings, machinery…)

LABOR – mental or physical work

Entrepreneurs use and combine these resources to make a profit while assuming the risk of running a business. Sustainability then comes into question mainly in the case of the first of the above mentioned, which is not only an important component of production and consumption but an essential asset we are obliged to preserve.

The primary purpose of land, water, air, sunlight, plants, and animals is not to assist us in making money but to serve all the beings on Earth to survive and thrive. Entrepreneurs should thus not only generate revenue and create value for their communities but also avoid any harm to the environment, or at least limit it to the absolute minimum.

Within our entrepreneurial tenure, we may experience loss or significant devaluation of these resources, which is the essence of the risk we're taking. That's why it is so important to consider them as one of the possible tools, not an ultimate and only goal.

INFORMATION

In the age of information technologies, the amount of data created every second is growing exponentially. The tech titans are accelerating this trend while reaping full advantage of its benefits. At the same time, not only multi-billion enterprises but also small and micro businesses are capable of harnessing the power of the Internet and data-driven applications to strengthen their position on the market. In fact, the access to the right type of data, their processing, communication, management, transfer, and storage, are fundamental factors in amplifying competitiveness of all modern—both for-profit and for-purpose—organizations.

As an entrepreneur, I work with a certain amount of time. On one hand, my time allowance is limited, on the other hand, I have full freedom to use it for my own benefit. Sometimes being faster means winning a deal. Sometimes taking my time results in a fulfilling experience or a better quality product. The responsibility to become a master of my time is mine and only mine.

As an entrepreneur, I depend on a constant flow of energy to think, to feel, to see, to understand, and to deliver the best outcome for me, my business, and my surroundings. Every single moment, I am aware of the things, people, and activities that charge me with energy, and I make considerate use of them. I know that energy means power, and this power is created within me.

As an entrepreneur, I never stagnate. I don't go to bed without progressing in any little way. I celebrate every small step forward in enhancing my health, knowledge, skills, and relationships. I don't wait for the perfect time to turn into a better person. My life is a continuous string of tiny improvements threaded one after another, to which I see no end.

As an entrepreneur, I am never alone. I understand that to ask, I need to give first. The more value I create for others, the stronger are the connections between me and my team, my business partners, friends, family, and my community. I choose with care the people I share my time with. The more I grow as a person, the more I attract those who hold the same values and beliefs.

As an entrepreneur, I use land, capital, information, and work of other people to build solutions that improve lives, address needs, and solve issues of my customers. I aim at increasing the value of my resources; my ultimate goal is, however, not a pure quantifiable profit. I know that money has so far not made the world a better place. I know that when my time is over, it won't help me to buy more of it. I know it has a limited ability to make me happy.

As an entrepreneur, I don't wait for external acknowledgment of my success. I move towards success by being an entrepreneur, day by day.

20. Who Is an Entrepreneur?

*E*ntrepreneurs are born imperfect like anyone else: they struggle and cry, flog themselves with doubts, and experience rejection considerably more often than they do praise. Yet, they don't give in to shame. They are survivors who manage to strike a fire in a wasteland. They keep the candle of dream burning in the middle of a shitstorm.

ENTREPRENEURS DON'T WAIT FOR THE PERFECT DAY.

They know that time is scarce, and the longer they wait, the less of it they have. They also know that the perfect circumstances simply don't exist, so they don't rely on them. They create their own.

ENTREPRENEURS CONSIDER FEAR THEIR ALLY.

They don't let it approach too close, but they don't reject it either. Fear serves them as the augur of challenges looming ahead, so they can plan and prepare accordingly.

ENTREPRENEURS ARE NOT INTIMIDATED BY IMPERFECTION.

They have tasted the potent power of continuous improvement to which they see no end. Besides, they see imperfection as uniqueness that ought to be explored, and possibly appreciated, not merely denounced.

Shame is an enemy whose sole mission is to make them believe that they are not good enough. They pledge to either ignore or fight and ultimately defeat this great nemesis.

Big projects, big responsibilities, big resolutions, and big promises can be frightening and overwhelming. Instead of looking too far for too long, which may cause them to lose their balance, they focus on their feet to steadily put one ahead of the other.

Entrepreneurs feel successful when they wake up a bit of a better person than the previous day, and when they go to bed knowing that they have in some little way improved someone's life.

They have the skills, knowledge, and resolve to meet the needs of others and address their most pressing issues. They don't primarily create products or offer services—they build sustainable solutions.

They understand that whatever we think about the world we live in is a work of fiction. They have faith in themselves to control their thoughts and emotions and to create their experience regardless of external conditions.

Entrepreneurs are fueled by self-improvement.

By constantly improving themselves, through learning, correcting their past mistakes, enhancing their physical health, and attaining spiritual balance, they make themselves better suited to deliver positive impact on society.

Entrepreneurs share their knowledge and skills whenever they can.

The inherent purpose of knowledge is for it to be shared. Some information and some skills give entrepreneurs a competitive advantage, so they naturally aim at knowing more or performing better than their peers. However, whenever it is possible, they also use their knowledge and skills to create a value that benefits not only themselves.

Entrepreneurs are truthful to themselves in their beliefs, actions, and passions.

Since our time on Earth is absolutely limited, we need to listen to our hearts, or intuition if you wish, now and then, to be able to tell if we are on the right path. Entrepreneurs try not to lie to themselves because they know that a (wo)man can be either their own greatest ally or their own greatest enemy.

Entrepreneurs are not perfect.

They don't have special super powers. They are just like anybody else. What makes them stand apart is their firm determination to avoid stagnation at any cost. They don't improve themselves to show off or prove their worthiness. They know that to grow is to be in control.

Entrepreneurs are fighters.

But they are not reckless. They cautiously choose their battles since they may consume a lot of their valuable energy. They also know when it is time to recede, rest, and prepare for the battles that are truly worth fighting for.

Entrepreneurs have purpose.

When they invest their time, energy, and skills into building something or serving someone, they know to what end.

Entrepreneurs don't always believe their eyes and ears.

To hear is not the same thing as to listen. To look is not the same thing as to see. To become a good listener, or a good observer, an entrepreneur needs to practice patience, focus, and concentration.

Entrepreneurs are problem solvers.

For an entrepreneur, there is no such thing as a problem without a solution. The solution may take time, discipline, a new skill, more resources, or a helping hand to be revealed, but it's always somewhere out there.

Entrepreneurs don't wait for opportunities to knock on their doors.

They keep their lives firmly in their hands, and they create success from within. Opportunities never appear out of the blue; one needs to make the first few steps and meet them halfway. That's why entrepreneurs observe, listen, and grow every day to find the right path.

Entrepreneurs embrace responsibility for their own education.

It doesn't matter if they had access to the best universities or if they couldn't afford to attend school. Entrepreneurs know where to look for available resources to build up their knowledge and strengthen their skills.

Entrepreneurs trust themselves to make uncertain decisions.

Often, they need to jump off the cliff blindfolded. Most of the time, they land on a safety net, which they had built for such cases over the previous years. Still, sometimes they shatter their bones. Then they use the recovery period to learn, and they are grateful for such a valuable lesson.

Entrepreneurs avoid seeing themselves as victims.

They don't try to control everything that happens around them or to them. Yet, they aspire and strive for full control over their mind and personal growth. If something goes wrong, they don't blame anything or anyone else for their feelings.

Entrepreneurs wear many hats.

When they are lost, they turn into adventurers. When they get beaten, they turn into fighters. When they fail, they turn into explorers.

ENTREPRENEURS ARE NEITHER BUSY NOR IDLE.

Entrepreneurs don't know the feeling of being bored. They have always something to do, and they usually know why they do it. At the same time, while busyness is a badge of honor for others, it's a sign of failing for them. They value their time, and they avoid wasting it by filling their days with endless tasks and meetings that don't produce relevant results.

ENTREPRENEURS ARE MASTER LISTENERS.

The overarching mission of entrepreneurs is to build solutions that address needs of other people. That's why, more than anything else, they do their best to ask good questions and decipher underlying messages in the answers they might receive.

ENTREPRENEURS SHAPE THE WORLD AROUND THEM.

When they decide they are bound to be successful, and they invest a substantial amount of their inner energy into this faith, the success eventually follows. When they see themselves as the person they want to be—and they cherish this self-image without doubt—the others inevitably start seeing them in the same way.

ENTREPRENEURS ARE OPTIMISTS.

They don't consider optimism to be a passive or naïve belief that "everything will turn out well in the end." Optimism has a deep individual meaning for them with a clear view of the desired outcome. They consider it ceaseless hard work rather than a panacea for the pains of everyday reality.

Entrepreneurs embrace failure.

For a brave entrepreneur, failure is nothing more and nothing less than an opportunity to learn.

Entrepreneurs are flexible.

Changing one's opinion is not a shame. Changing one's priorities is not a crime. Changing one's strategy is not a failure. And uncertainty is not an enemy. Things change, people change, including entrepreneurs themselves. When the world seems to disappoint, they pause, take a deep breath, and look around closely to find a new, better way.

Entrepreneurs are not afraid to get exposed.

They know that strength lies in vulnerability. Only when you're brave enough to be seen naked, to make mistakes, to blunder, can you achieve higher and reach farther than anyone else.

Entrepreneurs value their time more than anything.

When you lose money, you simply go back to providing value to other people so you can earn some more. On the other hand, when you lose time, there's no way to retrieve it back. You can always be richer. However, one day you will be about to die and none of that money will buy you extra time.

Entrepreneurs don't feel guilty for having fun.

They've heard the phrase "no pain, no gain" countless times (and sometimes even uttered it themselves), and they do work really hard to build the life of their dreams. Yet, they don't dismiss pleasure, since it helps them recharge energy and boost their creativity.

ENTREPRENEURS BELIEVE IN CHANGE.

True change never happens overnight, that's why entrepreneurs swear by everyday piecemeal improvement and innovation, even on the smallest scale. By nature they are patient because they see what others don't, which is that even though you can hit a stone hundreds of times without leaving a scratch on it, one day it may crack open.

ENTREPRENEURS CONSIDER MONEY A TOOL, NOT A PURPOSE.

Often their businesses make them wealthy, often they give up a portion of their revenue or personal income for the sake of sustainability. In any case, for them, money is simply a tool of exchange, not an ultimate goal. Since they believe in continuous improvement, they know that they are always able to provide value to others and make some more.

ENTREPRENEURS CAREFULLY PICK PEOPLE THEY SURROUND THEMSELVES WITH.

People can be either beneficial or detrimental to the energy level of a successful entrepreneur. People can also either help them grow or drag them down.

ENTREPRENEURS ARE NOT SHY TO SEEK HELP.

When they ask people and hear no, they don't feel ashamed. They simply find another person and ask again. When they are stuck in their minds, they look for help everywhere around.

They open their ears and eyes, listen and observe, and have faith in themselves that the right solution will come.

ENTREPRENEURS DON'T SEEK SHORTCUTS.

Easy roads don't always lead to the best results. Entrepreneurs focus on managing their time wisely, growing their productivity, and increasing the quality of their working life. But they don't hurry at every cost because sometimes only the rockiest journey can lead them to their desired destination.

ENTREPRENEURS DON'T ASK ANYTHING BACK.

When they help others, they do so because it's right, and they don't expect to be paid back. If they receive something back, though, they accept it without shame or false humbleness because meaningful relationships are essential both for their personal and business growth.

ENTREPRENEURS ARE NOT FEARFUL OF REJECTION.

Hearing "no" doesn't have any impact on their self-esteem, as it doesn't mean anything else for them but a signal to move on and find better ways to achieve what they want.

ENTREPRENEURS DON'T DEFINE THEMSELVES BY WHAT OTHERS THINK OF THEM.

Sometimes they are ridiculed, laughed at, and misunderstood. Often, their efforts earn but indifference or rejection. Then they weather these moments knowing that they are doing their best in every aspect of their lives: their work, their personal growth, and their relationships. When others show disrespect, it hurts, but it doesn't break them. Whereas if they were untruthful to themselves, they would become weak, and eventually surrender.

21. String of Beads

*I*s entrepreneurship all about changing the world? And what does that even mean? Is change needed and expected at all?

It is needed as long as you believe that you should have control over your (better) future and the future of those you care about. But we should not presume that our ultimate duty is to grow into the costume of a hero who makes everything happen within their short lifetime. To become the one person who shall "save the day" is an overwhelming, if not daunting, vision for most people. And that's why, in the end, most people give up on changing anything for themselves or anyone else. They are convinced that their potential feats of good would not be big or significant enough to make any difference.

You. Should. Not.

Being an entrepreneur is not about earning a certain amount of money, building a corporation of a certain size, or achieving a certain level of fame. It is about stringing beads of small, daily improvements on a thin thread that leads to lasting value and fulfillment. It is a way of life. It is a set of beliefs. And it is a window of opportunity to impact people's lives and contribute to a better society as a whole.

We have governments, armies, trade unions, corporations, international organizations, and powerful financial institutions. Why should we try moving things in
the right direction on our own?

Because an entrepreneur doesn't wait. He or she doesn't
expect anybody or anything to solve a problem for them. Perhaps there are entities or people who are more capable or
resourceful. But if their imminent priorities avoid addressing
a public issue or meeting needs of particular people, we rely
on entrepreneurs who possess the much-needed resolve,
skills, knowledge, experience, and tools to devise a solution,
albeit imperfect.

Entrepreneurs are strong individuals who are fit for survival. When it is in the interest of some privileged groups to
leave selected communities, or even states, in underdevelop-
ment, turmoil, or passivity, people depend on entrepreneurs
in their midst to design solutions to the most pressing social,
economic, and cultural challenges.

These innovators and change-makers can run various ven-
tures, from multi-billion-dollar companies, to one-(wo)man
shops, or local grassroots non-profits, yet what makes them
belong to one breed is their striving for excellence. Not out
of vanity, but out of responsibility, they always aim high, not
only with regard to their work, but also to their individual
growth and their legacy.

Entrepreneurs aim at raising funds as well. As managers,
they cultivate their teams, as leaders, they inspire, and as
businessmen or businesswomen, they develop goods and

services, or engage in trade, that generates revenue. They prefer to be self-sufficient, to say the least, and once they create jobs for others, they will focus on overall sustainability. If their businesses or projects fail to sustain themselves and their employees in the long term, it's hard to advocate for their existence. However, entrepreneurs are also driven by a purpose, which is often based on the values they share with a community of people they're fighting for.

As an entrepreneur, you may be mocked, you may be admired, you may be envied. You may inspire people, or you make them uncomfortable by disrupting their original patterns of thinking. All in all, as an entrepreneur, you're needed. You're not expected to be a hero. You were born to be of value to others.

Purpose

22. The Lost Piece

Imagine a box of thousands of jigsaw puzzle pieces appears at your doorstep. There's no instructions, no image to help you get started. You can't but spread the whole thing on the table and try to randomly fit the pieces together.

One by one.

It takes a while before you get the first hint of what you may see when you're finished. And even then, there are still countless more to connect.

Often it seems as if you have reached an impasse. So you need to start all over.

Again and again, and again.

Sometimes you have doubts if you will ever be able to complete the work.

Is it you or is the puzzle just too difficult? Is it even worth it? What if one of the pieces got lost?

The truth is that none of them are missing. They are all there, in front of your eyes, waiting for you to pick them up and put them in their right place.

Rushing won't help you. You simply need to stay focused and patient.

You are curious and determined.

So you do.

Then eventually, some long time later, what was originally a huge pile of random ordinary cutouts becomes a stunning masterpiece where everything is exactly where it is supposed to be. And you realize that you have actually seen that painting before.

Perhaps in your dreams.

What is our purpose and why should we keep looking for it? Are we ever going to learn if we are on the right path?

The answer is yes. We can. Because when we do, when we reach it, we get permeated with an unusual sensation that MAKES US FEEL REAL. We don't place any (self-restrictive) value, neither positive nor negative, on anyone else's opinions and behavior. We are truthful to ourselves, which is the only thing that seems to matter. We are confident that we are where we are supposed to be, doing what we are supposed to be doing.

There is no past and no future. Only now.

When we live for the future while constantly carrying the burden of our past, we never rest. We can never see what is there, right in front of our eyes.

The purpose of our living is inseparably linked to our core values. When we seek what brings us joy but contradicts our values, we never come close to satisfaction. There's always a better job, better salary, better partner... a better life that has slipped through our fingers.

That's why purpose is the only genuine concept, next to love. The rest is relative.

However, as it usually goes, the best things in life are hardly ever easy to get. Easy roads are prone to be clouded with deception. That's why purpose is difficult to find, and even more difficult to follow.

When we follow it, we're rewarded. We attract the right people we want to have in our lives. We find solutions to seemingly unsolvable problems. We attain unshakable inner strength.

When we betray it, we're taught a lesson. We lose our way while chasing remedies for the wounds on our self-esteem. We search for pleasure without ever being satisfied. We never attain full control.

A purpose gives us stability. It's an anchor in the boisterous oceans of our existence. It gives meaning to our actions, and it doesn't require to be understood.

A purpose is not the same thing as a passion, but our passions, in all their variety, nurture our purpose.

A purpose is not the one thing that can make us happy either. The one missing piece. No. It's all the pieces of one human life assembled in a way that they form a whole perfect picture.

23. Banning the Red Pen

hen we were little, we were close to our purpose.

Even though children rarely look into the meaning of their existence. It's not that their brains are not developed enough for such an intellectual deliberation. They are simply aware of their needs, and they know exactly what they want. It may seem just like the complete opposite, though, because now and then they struggle with expressing themselves in a way that would be comprehensible to us adults.

Often they also develop a special talent, skill, or a particular gift that feels completely natural... until a moment when some other human being stifles it with an ill-timed comment or a lack of emotional support.

Now, you might be thinking something like, "Well, I wanted to be an astronaut as a child, and now I'm pretty sure that it was not my purpose in life."

Maybe not, maybe you were not meant to become an astronaut. But you were not supposed to be told otherwise either. A child believes that he or she can do practically anything. There is no limit to their imagination.

And that is it. THE BOUNDLESSNESS. The non-framed blank canvas of their lives ahead.

As they grow and mature, they fill their canvases with new things, they improve the lines and explore what works and what doesn't. At the same time, the bigger, more experienced humans start to come in with their red pens. They cross whole parts out. They tell children what they should erase. They insist that they draw something more interesting, realistic, likable…

At that moment our canvases start shrinking. There are limits to honor. And we accept them because it feels somehow safer. Our canvas is not our own private space anymore. It is subject to the public eye. It is judged, evaluated. We are exposed, vulnerable. And it's not pleasant.

Approval, attention, acceptance, affection, appreciation… these, on the other hand, are.

The five As offer the much necessary guidance. They help us make decisions. And if we broke free from their demands, we would need to start responding solely to our bare selves… which is scary. Since childhood, we have learned to address our emotional needs based on interactions with others (they should like me, they should listen to me…). We have, however, failed to learn how to deal with our inner voice, and that is incomparably tougher.

Affection: How to love myself?

Approval: What is right and what is not?

Appreciation: How to value myself?

Acceptance: How to accept who I am?

Attention: How to meet my own needs?

But what if you are fundamentally wrong?

Unfortunately, there isn't a universal recipe. No shortcuts to happiness in sight. No guarantees. No immediate rewards for being good students of life.

That's why most people either give up or never strive to look for the reason of their being in the first place.

No wonder we hear people say, "I have everything I need… well, plenty of others are much less fortunate, so I can't really complain… just, something, I don't know, something is missing."

It's like when you stop yourself in the middle of searching for something, and you realize that you don't even remember what it was that you were looking for. Still, there's this irksome feeling that it was, indeed, important. Eventually, you give up and move on. Then, as time passes, the feeling occasionally comes back. But since you still can't recall anything, you choose to ignore it, until one day you ultimately forget.

If we're to avoid the sense of being lost, of being unfulfilled, we must start listening to ourselves, no matter how disturbing the things we hear at first may be. There is a voice in us, possibly rather muted by now, that has been trying to talk to us, to guide us. Always.

We need to look for that voice because it is our only true friend. Honest, straightforward, but kind.

It may take weeks, months, or years of daily practice, but one day we will recognize its calling once again. It will help us remember what we have been looking for. And our soul will be relieved.

What's more, we need to permit ourselves to make mistakes.

Have you "wasted" years of your life doing something that made you unhappy? Good. Try to be grateful for such an opportunity to learn and grow stronger. Have you failed, miserably, more than once? Well, then, embrace those failures as milestones on your journey. Try to understand their message, instead of reprimanding yourself that they ever happened.

Life gives us numerous hints along the way, although we tend to ignore them skillfully, until at some point it seems as if they have disappeared altogether. There are moments when it looks like the world has given up on us. Quite often, we give up on ourselves too. Yet, regardless of all that, there IS a reason for us to be here, on this planet, at this time. No matter if you choose to live up to it.

It's worth noting, though, that finding a purpose is not a goal to be achieved. It's how one decides to lead their life. Focusing on what is working and what has worked in the past. Looking for resources we have at hand, not for what is lacking. If something doesn't work, instead of asking, "Why me?" or "Why again?," ask, "How has it helped me?" or "What was I supposed to learn?"

After all, we can say that living in harmony with our purpose is a choice of lifestyle. The choice to look ahead.

24. More Of, Less Of

*P*urpose is not what people admire in us.

It's easy to fall into such a sweet trap, since we are all hungry after appreciation and approval. It makes us feel connected, important, and when we do feel that way, we develop a (dangerous) emotional addiction.

Since our childhoods, we have been painting our canvases and constructing our mental worlds based on the satisfaction of being seen by others in a favorable light.

> The most awful thing one can do to a person at their early age is to make them build impenetrable walls in their heads and, even worse, in their hearts.

Purpose is what makes people succeed and attain fulfillment.

SUCCESS

I'm doing what I want to be doing.

I'm where I want to be.

I'm with who I want to be.

I have what I need, and possibly what I want to have.

Yet, do we even know what we want to be doing, what we want to have, where we want to be and with whom?

When you ask people what they want to have more of or less of in their lives, they are usually able to come up with some answers. In contrast, the naked "WHAT DO YOU REALLY WANT?" leaves many bewildered.

It's in human nature to strive for the better. Better housing, better food. More comfort, more excitement. More money, more power.

More of what makes us feel good. Less of what makes us feel bad.

Fewer fights in the family, less friction with the partner. Less stress at work. Fewer failures that hurt one's self-esteem…

Still, it's not so much in human nature to fight for the best.

Wait, what?!

You may not agree right away since you've probably always aimed at the maximum you could get for yourself and your close ones. But have you always known what is just right? What is just enough?

The best you can get doesn't always mean the highest quantity of it. The best would be, in the ideal case, the optimum mix of what we look for in our life.

The LAW OF DIMINISHING RETURNS is a concept in economics which shows that when we increase a certain input in production (workforce, land, machinery, etc.), while the other factors stay constant, we will eventually reach a point (the point of diminishing returns) where each addition of the input yields progressively smaller increases in output. We can even reach a point (the point of negative returns) where the overall output decreases while we keep adding more input.

For example, imagine that we add fertilizer to the soil we use to grow vegetables. Up to a certain amount, the more fertilizer we add, the more vegetables we can grow. If we exceed that amount, though, the overall output will stop increasing progressively, and it can even decrease if we cause damage to the soil by over-fertilization.

The same goes for the consumption of goods. When someone is ravenous, eating two slices of bread will satisfy them more than eating only one slice. However, the incremental increase in their overall satisfaction between eating a fourth and a fifth slice of bread may not be as substantial as between the first and second one. If they eat a tenth slice, their overall pleasure may start decreasing, to the point when any extra chunk of bread would make them outright sick.

Let's look at our lives through the same lens.

When we sleep 7 hours instead of 4, we are more rested and focused. If we slept 13 hours, instead of feeling much better, we may become slow and lethargic.

When we decide to work 10 hours instead of 6 every day, we may see a rise in our productivity and our salary. The moment we work 16 hours per day, our productivity starts suffering, very likely also together with our health. If our salary or business revenue still keeps increasing with every extra hour invested, we need to evaluate if it compensates for the damage to our overall wellbeing.

When we learn something new, and practice on a regular basis, we experience improvement in substantial leaps. As we move on, the progress is not as striking as when we started. Then, one day, we hit a plateau when it seems we have stopped improving at all. Mostly, it doesn't mean we should stop learning; we simply need to find new methods, modify our plan, refocus on new areas, or take rest to refresh our mental and physical strength.

All in all, exploring what we want more of or less of in our life is a helpful technique to clarify our priorities and define strategies for personal and professional growth. Nevertheless, it's equally important to take into account the correlation between these individual life goals, and the extent to which "more of" one thing we want means "less of" another one we want as well.

For one person, influence and control are more relevant to their needs than family and free time. For another, a low level of stress and mental wellbeing are priorities ranking much higher than the numbers in their bank account.

Friends often tell us, "You can't have it all!" And most of the time it makes sense to us.

The thing about finding and following your life's purpose is that when you do, most of the other areas of your life which are important to you improve simultaneously and naturally along the way.

On the other hand, if you follow an alternative path (an immediate personal gain, interests or expectations of someone else, etc.), you will inevitably end up trading satisfaction in some areas of your life for dissatisfaction in others. Maybe you will even reach a point—the point of negative returns—when your efforts to build up your success would result in an overall decrease of your happiness.

There's a saying that goes, "It's better to be rich and healthy than poor and sick." Be that as it may, we know that pain and suffering don't spare those who are well-off and prosperous. Is then being sick and rich better than being sick and poor? And what about being sick, poor, and surrounded by family and friends who love and support you unconditionally, compared to being sick, rich, and getting the best medical care, yet knowing that no one really cares if you get better?

A WIN-WIN (positive-sum) GAME is a situation where all the participants profit in one way or another, usually by means of mutual cooperation. In simple terms, if you and I have a dispute, we aspire to solve it in a way that each of us gets what we have expected, and the overall outcome is positive.

Allow me to make an analogy here: FINDING PURPOSE MEANS REACHING A WIN-WIN STATE, in which we achieve our principal life goals—or are on the way to meeting them— while our overall satisfaction is relatively higher.

> How complex it sounds! I simply want to be successful and happy.

Well, it's not that complicated when you go back to listening to your inner voice, which guides you towards what you want in life. Or, instead, you could adopt certain behaviors, follow a particular philosophy, or resort to acts that would address your more immediate needs, such as the need for material comfort, security, variety, recognition, or praise. It'd probably be easier than to reveal your true purpose in life. Just bear in mind that a stellar career or wealth won't make you automatically less lonely. Or that developing a good social status, or even earning fame, doesn't necessarily bring about happiness or cement your self-esteem. Sometimes it works great. Sometimes it only feels that way, and when it does, we deal with a distorted, and highly addictive, perception. That's why, right from the beginning of our journey, we need to keep exploring what success means for us. What is it that we want? How can we tell we've achieved success if we cannot explain it either to others or to ourselves?

On the other hand, if we are able to define what success is to us, we will avoid a great deal of frustration, confusion, or even tears later down the line.

You should be aware of why you are where you are, why you're doing what you're doing, most of the time. You might be wrong at first, but without giving it a try, you won't ever find the right answer. Simply remember that making mistakes, even those giant and painful ones, is an all-important part of revealing the right road. The road you truly want to walk.

25. Fear of Failure

The difference between a mistake and a failure is this:

When you make a mistake, you can use the occasion to learn, to improve yourself, and avoid a similar, or worse, situation in the future.

When you stop learning, you fail.

It's really up to us to decide. Was it a mistake, a setback? A bad one, yet temporary? Is there something good that it has taught you? Is it worth it to keep going?

Or is it over? Is it that you don't want to learn, to grow anymore? Have you given up control altogether?

Sometimes we make mistakes that bring about serious consequences. People get hurt deeply. Lives of many are affected. We lose money, respect, friends. Our self-worth is in shatters. At that point, it's hard to say, "I made a mistake."

It sounds defiant, maybe even arrogant. Yet, AT THE BEGINNING OF BOTH A MISTAKE AND A FAILURE IS THE VERY SAME THING: A WRONG CHOICE, A WRONG DECISION. WHAT MATTERS, THOUGH, IS WHAT WE SEE AT THE END.

The end result of making a mistake is that a brand new decision is made, a decision to reduce the past and inevitable

mistake
[mi-steyk], noun
~ makes you stronger
failure
[feyl-yer], noun
~ makes you weaker

harm, and to do one's best to prevent any more harm, to both others and ourselves, in the future.

On the other hand, the product of a failure is an individual who has renounced their control over the situation and considers themselves a victim of the circumstances.

If you can't decide on the wording (a mistake, a blunder, a total disaster?)—which is completely natural, since, as a rule, our words tend to reflect the intensity and color of our short-lived emotions—then simply think and talk about the wrong choices you have made. Try to understand why they were wrong, or why they seemed right at that time. Come up with ways to deal with the consequences. Set up an action plan of the next steps. And most importantly, make sure you're motivated and determined to keep trying in the future.

> **Making mistakes, making wrong choices, is a sign of being human.**
>
> **Accepting responsibility for one's decisions is a sign of being a strong human.**

Why are we afraid of failure then?

In reality, for many people, their FEAR OF FAILURE is a stronger drive than the vision of success.

Just think about it. If you don't achieve what you want, you need to deal with the practical outcomes of your choices, or the "circumstances you couldn't influence" (you choose how you put it), e.g., living in an awful place, getting paid much less than you deserve, dating someone you can't trust... IS IT THEN THE SITUATION ITSELF YOU FEAR SO MUCH, OR

 What is worse: getting less of what you want, getting hurt, or the ultimate damage to your self-esteem?

The good news here is that we do hold control over our emotions to a certain extent, and we can learn to change them in an instant.

Emotions are a signal sent by our body for us to understand that something is wrong.

While some of them are born out of desires, instincts, or information stored in the unconscious part of our mind (i.e., we don't have direct access to them, and, as a result, we find it quite difficult to understand their message), others arrive as a consequence of our conscious analysis of the information that is received from our internal and external environment.

Therefore, as we have seen before, emotions can indeed be regulated with the help of our thoughts.

In simple terms: something happens (objectively a neutral event), we make a judgment about it (a thought with negative, neutral, or positive charge), and this judgment shows in our body as an emotion (fear, disgust, anger, sadness, joy, surprise, etc.).

If the feeling is unbearable, we may bury it into the unconsciousness, which, on the one hand, will give us temporary relief, but, on the other hand, will create problems for many years to come, since our body won't stop broadcasting signals (new distressing emotions, physical ailments, chronic diseases) in the hope that one day we understand their message.

That's why emotions as such are not inherently bad or good; they simply come off as subjectively pleasant or unpleasant.

If we tried to generalize the whole process, we could say that bad thoughts (destructive, harmful...) produce pain (unpleasant emotions), while good thoughts (creative, productive...) produce joy (pleasant emotions). And since like attracts like, through joy we attract what we desire into our lives, and through pain we attract what we fear. Including failure.

In sum, by changing what you think, you are able to lessen the overall amount of strain, pain, and stress that hurts you.

It's not easy. No doubt about that. It takes practice, and plenty of trials and errors. But the important thing to remember is that we are able to protect ourselves. Our bodies and minds have emergency mechanisms in place, which can help us any time we need them.

Human beings are extremely resilient. We know how to deal with pain. We are capable of rising from the ashes and starting all over again. But for some reason, the pain itself is not the thing we fear most. It is the judgment of those around.

We live our lives and run our businesses as if we constantly needed to prove ourselves. We compete with those around us. We compare ourselves with those who perform better than us in the game of life and feel disdain for those who don't.

That's correct. We spot and target weaknesses in other people because they remind us of what we can become, or what, deep inside, we believe that we already are.

You may have noticed that individuals with sound self-esteem and natural confidence rarely look down on others. They are also not inclined to compare themselves to them. It's because when you are aware of your own value and of what you bring to the world, you don't need endorsement. Besides, weaknesses and losses of other people don't threaten you.

We always focus on what is important to us, what we care about.

Let's imagine a beautiful, well-dressed woman walking into a room. One person would notice her amazing shoes—she spots them right away because she is a bit of a fashionista herself. Another person would directly stare at her rounded hips—he sees the body, rather than the clothes, because that's what is on his mind more often than anything else. A third person's first thought would be how superficial that woman must be—right away, he uses her appearance to judge her personality, possibly because his own intellect is something he is concerned about, although he may not realize it or admit it to himself, let anyone else.

What we give to others is what we expect to receive.

When I judge, I worry about being judged. Judgments and opinions of others mirror my own. That's why I take things personally. Even though on the surface I am convinced I'm defending myself against the other, the truth is I'm defending myself to myself.

I expect people to see me as I see myself, which is rather a valid point. So if I condemn myself for failing, people around will start sniffing at me.

THE ANTIDOTE TO FAILURE IS VALUE:
a) My own value
b) Value I provide to others

Do you know who you are and do you accept yourself fully? Do you strive to be better every day? Do you aim at creating value, in whatever you do?

If yes, then you cannot fail. You will make wrong choices, that's inevitable. But they should not make you believe that you're not good enough. That you're not worth it—worthy of being appreciated, worthy of being liked, worthy of being seen.

Often the pressure is almost unbearable. The unimaginable consequences of a single bad move.

It is not easy and it will never be. But then, isn't hardship ingrained in the skin of every entrepreneur?

As an entrepreneur you agree to assume a substantial responsibility, since your job is not only to make money but also to make lives of other people better. You respond to your partners, to your employees, investors, customers, your family, and likely also to local communities and other parties that are affected by your activities.

That's a lot to take for a single individual.

Your words and acts can have a substantial impact, which is amazing and terrifying at the same time. That's why learning is such an important element of being a successful entrepreneur.

You need to keep learning to predict, avoid, or rectify mistakes you make. Yet, the prospect of making them should not paralyze you.

It's impossible to be perfect. It's impossible to be always right. We can but let it go and aim for the best. We can work on our ability to get up faster when we fall. We can remind ourselves of our unique value to the world.

An awareness of our self-worth is an essential component of our ability to succeed. It is an integral part of the definition of what success means to us. Even though our actions affect others, at the end of the day, we only have ourselves to answer to.

Entrepreneurship takes a lot of courage and even more confidence. But you know what they say:

"YOU DON'T NEED CONFIDENCE TO DO SOMETHING. YOU NEED TO DO SOMETHING TO GAIN CONFIDENCE."

26. What Makes Your Heart Sing?

*W*hy were we brought to this Earth?

How does one reveal their purpose?

Is there a meaning to anything we do?

Aren't these questions too difficult to answer? Too abstract maybe?

Whatever your impression on the matter is, if you at least tentatively accept the fact that you have a mission to fulfill, you may (perhaps subconsciously at first) start looking for some helpful indicia.

Whether you were meant to be an entrepreneur or not, you may look for the signs of what type of work, activities, interests, or relationships are those that bring harmony and fulfillment to your life.

On the other hand, if you choose to believe that your life doesn't have a purpose, you tend to adopt the mindset of a victim. You assume that most of the things that happen to you are out of your control.

Such a mindset proves to be rather comfortable at times, but, be that as it may, it's still important, and much worth it, to find a path that will make sense to you and that will lead you to the life you want.

My favorite expression is, "It makes my heart sing." It brings our focus directly to the right place and makes us contemplate the right type of feelings. It's the perfect starting point for our exploration.

> Can you remember a moment or an activity that made your heart sing?

Now, you will often hear that you cannot build your business solely around your passions. Needless to say, the essence of a successful company is its capacity and resolution to address needs of its potential customers.

How do all these things add up then?

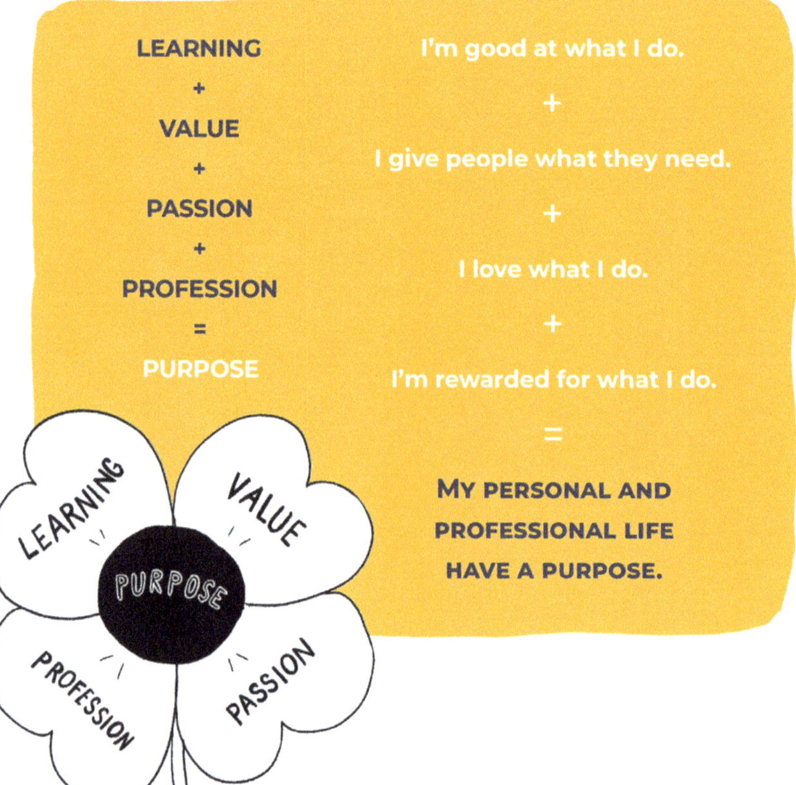

Living according to our purpose starts with CONTINUOUS SELF-IMPROVEMENT, so we are able to deliver value both to ourselves and to others.

That being said, it's not necessary, or even common, to wait for the perfect moment, the moment when you know just everything, in order to start building your own business. First, there's arguably no such thing. Second, learning doesn't have a beginning or an end. Or let's rather say, it starts with your birth and ends with your death. It's a process. It's a choice of life.

The primary skill we need to develop at this point is LISTENING. If we aim to be entrepreneurs, we need to become really good listeners, so we can identify the needs of other individuals. Then, besides developing our listening skills, we should also keep nourishing our CREATIVITY, so we can solve the issues we come across better than anyone else.

When you keep improving yourself and aim at solving problems for people around you, or address their pressing needs with new, innovative solutions, you can call yourself an ENTREPRENEUR.

Yet, people are often really good at something, with others making good use of their skills or knowledge, however, the joy of doing so is missing. That's why passion—or in simpler terms: doing what you like to do—is so important for us to cultivate. Passion is a fire that keeps us motivated and pushes us forward when things get hard.

When you are good at what you do and what you do is what people want, you're an entrepreneur. When you are good at what you do, you give people what they want, and you truly enjoy doing it, then you're a HAPPY ENTREPRENEUR.

Lastly, if we believe entrepreneurship is our calling, rather than getting a regular job, we may consider stepping up the game. Running a business is about practical problem solving and strategic execution, and one doesn't need to run a registered corporation to become an entrepreneur. However, most people opt for an official legal entity because it helps them scale efficiently.

Doing business assumes being paid for what you have to offer. There's a sufficient demand, i.e., a group of people (large enough to sustain your business model) in need of something that you can provide, ideally at a better quality, faster, or cheaper than any close alternative or the product of your direct competition.

So, the quest after delivering value, to both ourselves and others, doesn't end here, rather the opposite. If we aspire to succeed as entrepreneurs, we should start developing our leadership and management skills. What's more, if we aspire to be good managers, we should also facilitate educational and training opportunities to the people we work with.

Simultaneously, it's essential that we incorporate validation and testing processes into our operations, so our products or services comply with the needs and expectations of our clients. In a nutshell, we have to KEEP ASKING QUESTIONS, of both our customers and ourselves: "What do people need? Can I fulfill those needs better than anyone else? Where is room for improvement?"

Therefore, if you are good at what you do, and deliver a high-quality product or service that other people not only want but they also pay you for, you're a PROFITABLE ENTREPRENEUR.

At this point, the voice of passion in us often gets hushed up. We have responsibilities that make us sweat at night. We face formidable challenges on a daily basis. The question "Do I enjoy what I do?" is not on the menu of our personal growth anymore.

The stress of keeping up with everything that needs to be done often makes our hearts stop singing altogether.

Don't let that happen.

Money comes and goes. Businesses open and close, but you have only one life. And even if your passion is not what pays your bills, you need to keep such a fire in you burning. Only then will your spirit speak back to you. Only then can you trust your intuition, your inner wisdom.

The strong person you may become as a result would make decisions that can lead to building something with a purpose in itself. Such person will also know when it is the right time to stop and move on. They will not hold onto things that attract prestige and financial gain while unable to close a gaping void in their soul that makes them ask one obnoxious question night and day. That question goes:

What is missing?

27. What Is Missing?

As far as what is missing in our lives, we all have priorities at any given time. As a rule, though, we navigate towards pleasure, and we run away from pain.

The fastest routes to pleasure are quite conventional, such as food, sex, or entertainment. This leads to shocking statistics in terms of overweight and obesity in various countries. In the same way, new technologies make sexually satisfying materials so widely accessible that more and more people daily spend long hours in front of a screen, free from the effort (daunting for many, these days) of finding a real partner.

At first, we always look for what is readily available, fast, and easy.

Children aren't more attached to their smartphones than to anything else just because they have no better options at hand. Even though teenagers especially would rarely admit it, affection, approval, and recognition from parents and friends would mean so much more to them. Yet, these are sometimes hard to get, and when a child feels unnoticed, unloved, unvalued, the Internet gives them instant gratification ranging from fun content to virtual communities and worlds they can hide themselves in.

Besides, even the little ones notice quite early on that many pleasurable things in life are not out there for free.

They hear from their parents: *You can't have it because we don't have enough money. I can't play with you because I need to work (to pay for your school, toys, etc.). If you don't study, you will never get a good job, and without a good job, you won't earn enough to buy what you want...*

We learn from the outset that money is important. With money, we can buy stuff that makes us feel good. Money gives us security and reduces dependence on others. It offers freedom and much wider portfolio of life choices. That's why it often becomes a paramount goal to pursue.

Now, there is not so much wrong with money per se and neither with our pursuit of it. THE PROBLEM IS THAT THE AMOUNT OF PLEASURE MONEY CAN BUY AT ANY GIVEN MOMENT IS LIMITED.

In theory, and for many in practice, it's possible to grow richer and richer. Yet, somehow we are hardly ever fully satisfied. We could always use more money, to have more of X or better Y.

While there are people who are nothing but greedy and don't necessarily consider what they seek to accumulate as a path to pleasure (actually, the accomplishment of having "more of" might be pleasurable in itself), most of us fail to have just enough because the pleasure associated with things we can buy is never permanent.

A lasting sense of satisfaction, on the other hand, stems from finding our purpose in life, from contributing and being connected to others, and possibly from loving and being loved. Anything we earn and spend on extra pleasure then is a bonus we enjoy but don't cling to.

People, in general, tend to believe that achieving material comfort is the safest route to an enjoyable life experience. Yet, we keep seeing wealthy people resorting to drugs, alcohol, or other self-destructive behavior, since money can't close every gaping void in a human soul.

Is it then possible to make money and at the same time follow a purpose that is close to one's heart?

Certainly it is if:

1. We offer certain value to others

2. We never cease improving ourselves

3. We nourish our passion and creativity

Power and a sense of personal significance perform some-what better in regard to replacing our true purpose. When we feel important, we assume our life has a meaning, which at times may be the case.

When our core values are not aligned with what we do, some form of inner tension is being built up, which may cause "inexplicable" stress and, as a result, lead to chronic health issues.

For some individuals, and some businessmen or busi-nesswomen, power is a strong drive and an intoxicating medicine for their self-esteem. But when is it completely self-serving and when can it be used for attaining an actual positive impact?

Some people have comparatively more power than others, which is a fundamental basis for social stratification. Power, in terms of relations between people, is the ability of an individual to influence decisions and behavior of other individuals. It is associated with authority (whether forced or natural), control (over resources, people, etc.), and leadership.

If one's purpose in life is to become a leader, their power and their capacity to control and influence others needs to be channeled into creating a safe environment which:

a) fosters growth of the whole group, community, or organization,

b) stimulates personal growth of its members, and

c) encourages collaboration and mutual respect.

LEADERS MOVE PEOPLE TO ACTION AND INSPIRE CONFIDENCE AND MOTIVATION TO ACHIEVE A COMMON GOAL.

The need to influence others ranks high among other human needs, alongside the need for significance. Feeling significant is satisfying, and it can often overdrive our search for purpose.

It's in our nature to compare ourselves to others. When our brain receives a signal that we are better at something, or that others look to us with respect, awe, or even fear, it triggers a huge boost to our inner self-image.

Such a strategy is a fairly risky and shaky one. In fact, a self-image that is built upon weighing ourselves against other people and driven solely by recognition and approval needs constant reinforcement. It is so fragile that any event in our lives that states otherwise (we're not good enough, we've failed, people judge us, reject us...) can shatter it to thousands of pieces in a matter of seconds.

If you opt for a similar journey, be prepared for it to be an exhausting one. On the other hand, if your sense of significance is naturally linked to fulfilling the mission you have taken up in this life, you can expect peace to enter both your mind and your body.

Having said that, let's not forget the old good affection. We should not derive our decisions and choices exclusively from expectations and responses of other people. Still, feeling accepted and loved is something we humans all long for.

> Love and purpose don't contradict each other. They are conjoined twins who cannot survive on their own if separated.

The big word "love" makes a good number of you cringe as it evokes a fairytale-like romance, a scathing passion... or something that exists only in the land of fantasy. But love can stand for the bonds we have in our family or a strong link between two best friends. Love is a relationship of unconditional acceptance of the other person as they are, a relationship of respect, of reciprocal support.

In the moments when it seems that there is something fundamentally wrong with our lives, we either tend to blame others or we directly move onto blaming ourselves. For not being enough. For making yet another wrong decision, for trusting yet another wrong person. For allowing ourselves to be vulnerable.

And here we are! Hurt, failed, humiliated. We've given so much and we've received so little. What is wrong with us?

We try hard to walk through life with our heads up. And yet, sooner or later, we end up on our knees, spitting dirt. Drained, a bit sadder, a bit wiser. Disappointed.

Do we have any control whatsoever? Are we damned?

Our heart is bleeding, and our mind is flashing with an unknown error. The pain edges on unbearable, and our survival instinct commands us to mute it as of now.

What do we do?

We may try not to feel at all. Numb ourselves with the excess of work, drinks, food, sex, sports, TV, online (social) entertainment… We either keep ourselves extremely busy and distracted, or we fall into complete lethargy, convinced that the best way to survive is to do nothing.

If we ever had the patience for some serious soul-searching, and if we drilled deep enough, we would most probably hit upon THE ABSENCE OF PURPOSE OR LOVE. The result of which is the impression that no matter what we do, no matter how hard we try, things are always somehow out of order.

For many people, it's their faith that presents a fixed point they can hold onto. They know their God loves them and has the right path laid out for them.

This is actually quite crucial. People who believe know that such a path exists. This belief helps them overcome difficult times. There is a meaning, there is an order, which comes from somewhere beautiful that goes far beyond them.

People who don't believe in something greater than them need to rely on their own capacity to make some sort of purpose materialize in their lives.

Here, the belief in purpose is similar to the belief in God.

It doesn't make pain stop appearing, uninvited. Pain will still be felt, mistakes will still be made, bridges burnt, tears shed, relationships broken.

However, if we seek purpose, we embrace these moments as a part of the journey. For a journey that is smooth and void of hardships doesn't exist.

The sweeter the goal awaiting us at the end, the thornier the road we walk on.

When we don't have a purpose in mind, doubts cloud our minds and despair weakens our hearts. On the contrary, if we actively search for one, or if we've already found it, the pain we go through as a result of our temporary failures is not strong enough to make us give up. We don't end up pitying ourselves. We treat ourselves with care, as if we were going through an illness that is irritably unpleasant but will fade away soon. We know that we're where we're supposed to be and that we will ultimately attract the right opportunities and the right people who will stand by our side when we achieve exactly what it is we deserve to have in our lives.

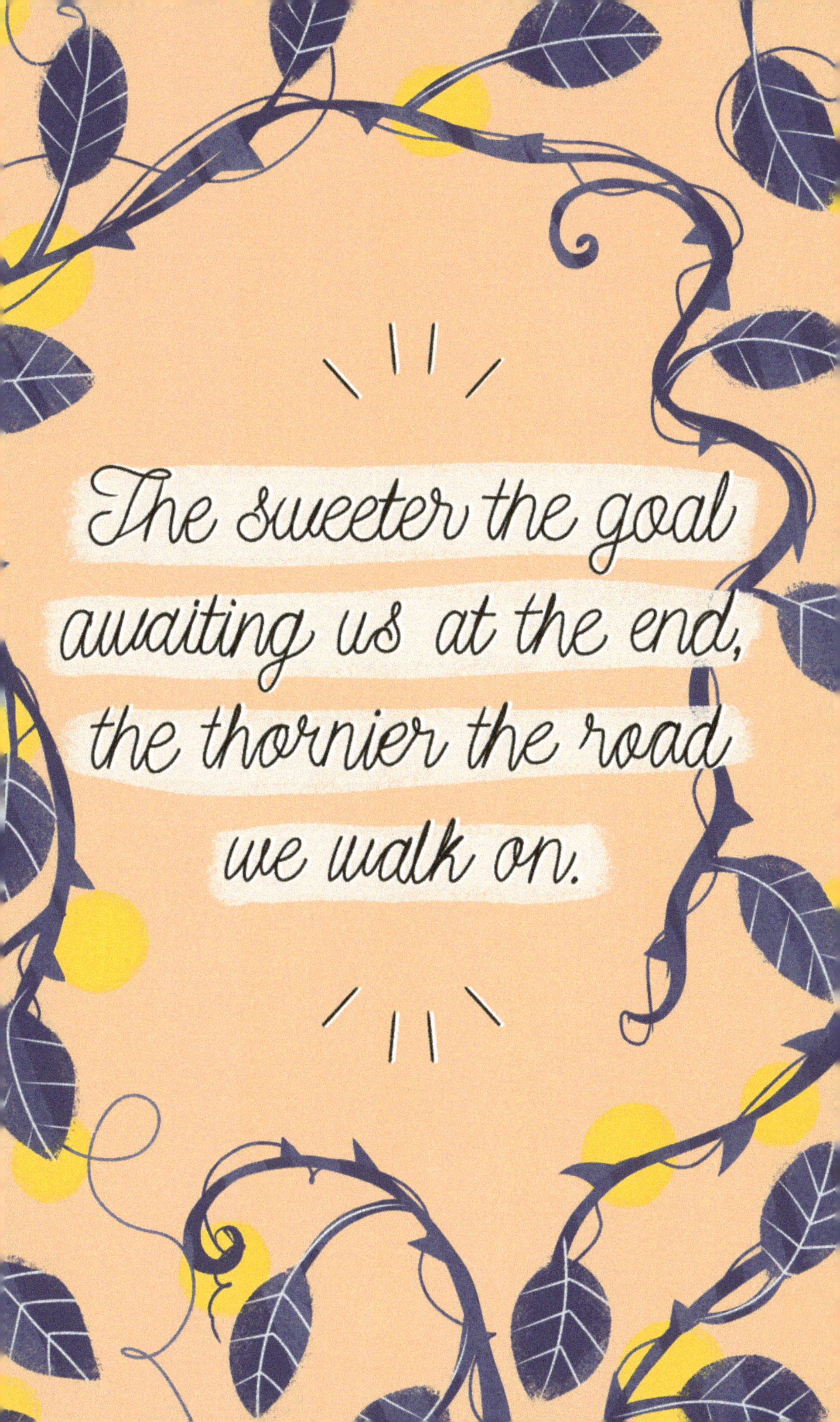
The sweeter the goal
awaiting us at the end,
the thornier the road
we walk on.

Control

28. The Importance of Time

A sense of being in control is characteristic for its tendency to routinely slip through our fingers. Besides, when we attempt at winning it back, we often forget that the place to start with is our perception and our management of time.

Even though perception is highly subjective and time as such doesn't let itself be managed, we can accomplish substantial shifts in our personal and professional lives when we use the time we have in a much better way. Time feels abstract and abundant, that's why we often ignore its importance as a fundamental resource and a tool to get what we want. At best, we run after getting done as much as possible in as little time as possible, i.e., filling the passing time units with the greatest amount of a desired activity.

Time is:

A) RELATIVE

Every individual perceives time in their own way, at any given moment. For two different people, who are simultaneously at the same place, one hour can feel either like an eternity or a finger snap.

When we're absorbed in an activity we love, we may lose the sense of time entirely—the reality appears timeless. When we suffer, each minute drags along at a snail's pace.

B) LINEAR

In the minds of people inhabiting the Earth, time seems to be linear. Our civilization has yet to learn about its other dimensions.

Things have their beginnings and their ends. At one given moment, we're born (we start existing), and at another moment, we die (we cease to exist).

C) OMNIPRESENT

Time affects everything, on both personal and professional levels.

Even though we prefer to believe that time is tied to the quantity of what we do, it has a much more profound impact on its quality.

We can escape from space, but we can't escape from time.

D) FINITE

On an individual level, the time we have from the moment we are brought into this world until some point in the future when we die is absolutely limited.

With every second passed, our time allowance diminishes. Besides, we use our time, or we outright waste it, without knowing how much we have left.

Every moment passed is irretrievable... never to be gotten back again... gone.

We can live every single moment only, and only once.

29. Variety of Choice

On a global level, the life expectancy has been steadily rising. In many countries, this fact can be attributed to better medical care, higher standards of hygiene, or access to nutritious food.

On the other hand, one may ask: DO WE REALLY LIVE LONGER?

Within the Western civilization, particularly, the common values have shifted significantly towards individual achievements and comfort, which means we rush through our lives, never entirely satisfied with what we currently have and what we've accomplished.

More people choose to remain single because the institution of marriage and family, which formerly offered not only emotional but also economic support, is hindering their career trajectory and jeopardizing their choice of lifestyle. An increasing number of couples lose interest in conventional relationships, and either they meet up to enjoy the occasional physical interchange or, on the contrary, they don't trouble themselves with having sex altogether. Birth rates are falling in numerous developed countries, and so far no efficient model on how to deal with the aging population has been designed.

Furthermore, the way we communicate has changed profoundly in the past decades.

We don't call anymore, we text. Words are being replaced with images. On one hand, we are more connected than ever. A business team can work remotely, spread out to all four corners of the globe, using only virtual channels to talk to each other. Family members can keep in touch when traveling thanks to video chat. Social networks enable us to follow the private lives of a vast number of people. We can get hold of practically anyone anywhere in the world.

On the other hand, when a group of friends meet for a coffee, they won't spend their time together without checking their phones at least a few times throughout the conversation.

Why is that? Why is it that I agree to meet with someone, and once I face this person, they become much less interesting than what is happening in the Kingdom of the Internet?

Some call it the FOMO—Fear of Missing Out—which results from the possibility to stay connected to our personal and professional networks at all times. As a consequence, we are constantly afraid of missing an important message, notification, status, piece of content, new experience, or an interesting opportunity.

Then there's the fact that as far as our social life goes, the virtual reality is much safer for our fragile ego than the present reality. On the Internet, I'm who I choose to be. In reality, they see me as I am.

That's why, as soon as we sit by the table with someone, we pull out our phone to plug into the virtual world, in case the real interactions are not engaging enough, or even worse, if they are unfavorable to us in some way. When we're on our phone, tablet, or computer, we can end any interaction with one quick click. In reality, one simply cannot mute a person, disappear, or teleport oneself to a more appealing situation.

The choices of instant entertainment and gratification are almost limitless, and we've become spoiled. Our attention span ranges from seconds to minutes at maximum.

Like, don't like.

Swipe, switch.

Now, let's go back to the good old TV. Imagine you just spent an hour zapping through various channels because you couldn't choose which one to settle on. Eventually, if someone asked you how you have enjoyed the program, you would most probably feel rather dissatisfied.

Now compare this to the experience of watching one good movie, including your favorite food and drinks, together with a good friend. How would the whole experience differ from the first one?

OUR BRAINS LOVE A VARIETY OF CHOICES. It is one of the most basic human needs. At the same time, though, the more choices we have, the more difficult it is for us to make a final, most favorable decision, provided that the criteria for doing so are not clear.

If our goal is to lose weight, it's easy to choose between one healthy and one unhealthy meal. When we are offered five different healthy and tasty dishes, the decision-making becomes much harder. The major criteria are met (healthy + tasty), so what's next? With the choice of only five options, we might still manage. Let's say we would dismiss a salad if we feel like eating a warm meal. Then we would turn away a dish that contains pepper since we're allergic to it. In the end, we're left with three similar choices, so we go for our best bet of which meal will please our taste buds.

When we go to a movie theater, which offers six different movies of various genres, we may pick out one without much hesitation. When we open a website on our computer which allows us to stream a countless number of movies in our preferred category, we may find ourselves paralyzed by such an extensive choice. Now we're talking dozens or even hundreds of options.

If we're not completely sure, why wouldn't we simply choose one randomly? Here, the fear of missing out arrives on stage once again. WE INHERENTLY STRIVE FOR THE VERY BEST OPTION. When our mind senses that the criteria are too complex or fuzzy, it becomes confused. Either we give up on making any decision altogether, or we end up anxious or apprehensive of having missed a better alternative.

We can observe this phenomenon even in the domain of work productivity. Procrastination is nothing else than being carried away by a variety of choices of what we could or should be doing at a given moment.

It's not uncommon for us to postpone finalizing a certain task until a mere few hours before a deadline. Because then we are left with only two choices, either we get it done or we fail. Our brain picks up on this straightforward verdict and focuses all its resources on the preferred goal. Whereas if there's a week left to our deadline, there are many more criteria at play. One of them is what we actually enjoy and don't enjoy doing at a given moment. The further from the target date, the stronger the role it has. Our brain evaluates our fleeting emotions, other tasks to fulfill, momentary preferences... and if the criteria of urgency don't offer any help, it opts for something more pleasurable or less painful.

Again, the more options at hand, the higher the chances that we don't stick to one activity for long.

In short, the more doesn't always mean the better. Especially, if we talk about time.

In this century, we have more choices than we'd ever had before. As the new technologies advance in leaps and bounds, there are countless alternatives at hand of how we can pass our time. Technology is shrinking the world by enabling communication regardless of our physical presence. And technology also drives us apart by sucking away our attention.

The life expectancy is rising, yet it is no easier for us to deal with all those extra seconds, minutes, hours, days, weeks, months, and years. We like variety, but we don't like failing at making the right choice. A considerable number of people nowadays are seeking treatment for depression, anxiety, panic attacks, or other mental disorders. We live longer, but overall, we don't seem to be so much happier.

Time is finite and relative at the same time. If there is one solid certainty we have in life, it is that every moment passed is gone forever. However, THE HIGHER THE QUALITY OF THE MOMENT PASSING, THE RELATIVELY LONGER IT APPEARS.

INTELLIGENT USE OF TIME = HAVING CONTROL

That's why, in both our personal and professional life, we need to pay our respects to time as our primary resource to achieve the most desired goals.

30. Level Up

For entrepreneurs, the argument that good management of time means having control is valid all the more. Entrepreneurs often perceive time as their enemy or a rival who is hard to beat. Instead of cooperating with it, they work against it.

As an aspiring entrepreneur, you are required to execute a dreadful load of various jobs. You start at the zero level, which feels to be a bleak and hostile place. You would do anything to jump one step higher in no time. So you rush, multitask, and wear many hats to get your project going. You launch fast, fail fast, improve, repeat.

At this point, it seems there's a severe deficit of time in your day. You haven't learned yet how to prioritize.

Everything is important, EVERYTHING!

You're afraid that, if you slow down, you'll get crushed (by competition, by debt, by expectations of others, your own…).

Then, eventually, you do manage to mount a few levels. Up there, it doesn't look all that unfriendly anymore, mostly because you've gained a good dose of confidence along the way. While still breathing heavily, you allow yourself some rest. You analyze, reevaluate, strategize. You start learning to delegate, collaborate more, and communicate better.

Furthermore, for the first time, you consider time not as something to compete with but rather something to take advantage of, despite the fact that there are few to learn from. Time is hard to tame and most people you know struggle on a daily basis to make good use of it, just like you. Some go to bed defeated night by night. That's why you hear conflicting opinions.

> To succeed, you need to work hard—that is, log as many hours as possible. To succeed, you need to work smart—that is, work less but more efficiently. A work-life balance doesn't exist if you aim for the top business league. Pay attention to your leisure and family time or you will burn out pretty fast. Time is money. Time is more valuable than money. Time is free. Time is relentless.

Even though myriads of books and articles on time management and productivity are clamoring for your attention, it seems so hard to find the right model for your needs. You've mastered an army of business and managerial skills, many of which are indeed related to time. Fast customer service, efficient product development, streamlined logistics... How come you fail at something so elementary as having control over the time you have as an individual?

31. Full Time Control? Easily!

You can't claim full control over your life unless you learn to have full control over your time. It is a fundamental skill to master and it basically revolves around the following areas:

Productivity
Busyness
Habits
80/20 Principle
Free Time

PRODUCTIVITY

PRODUCTIVITY AS A CONCEPT POINTS TO HOW MUCH YOU CAN GET DONE IN A GIVEN TIME PERIOD. Create more, execute more, achieve more... perform better, higher, faster. Thousand of pages have been written on the subject, but in essence, it all boils down to:

1. Priority
2. Focus

1 – PRIORITY

Never skip this point if you want something major done. It's basically up to you if you prioritize your tasks and goals weekly or daily. In general, YOU SHOULD NOT GO TO BED

1a – TAKE NOTE

You can keep a small (the smaller the better) notepad or a pack of sticky notes on your bed table. Just before you call it a night, write down a few points of what you really, really need to get done the following morning. When you wake up, review the note, and put it in your pocket so you can cross out the tasks throughout the day. In the evening, just toss it away, and prepare a new one.

Or use an app—for making notes or tracking tasks—on your phone, tablet, or computer (obviously, not a good idea if you don't use it every day), in a similar manner. The advantage of a small piece of paper is that you can't fit much on it, so it will push you to think twice about your choices. The advantage of an app is that you can reshuffle the tasks easier, should your priorities during the day change.

Besides, most of us would rather lose a piece of paper, whereas we all make sure to have our phones with us wherever we go, even though this fact per se is normally detrimental to our productivity and focus.

1b – ORGANIZE

It's advisable to mark the significance and urgency of each task by listing them in an up-down manner. If the number of the individual duties you have on your plate is fairly high, and you don't want to miss any of them, you can divide them into:

ESSENTIAL
IMPORTANT
OPTIONAL

The essential ones are those that shouldn't be missed so you can call your day a success.

The important ones are those that need to be done, and you will do your best to have them done, but the world will not crumble if they slip through.

The optional tasks can include anything, including items related to your family or leisure time. You can mark them for yourself to remember, but you needn't feel guilty if you don't end up fitting them in.

Essential = SUCCESS
Important = Good job!
Optional = Bonus

Many apps will allow you to distinguish individual tasks by color, which can be a nice visual aid to orientate yourself throughout the day. If you use a piece of paper, the alternative is colored pencils or markers.

None of the three blocks should go beyond five items, though, especially the first two. As you become more advanced at managing your time, you will see that your "essential" list hardly ever goes over three tasks.

Advanced tip:

If your tasks repeat and you are getting the hang of organizing your daily schedule, you can write a small number next to each item, indicating your time estimate. It is especially useful for those who struggle with procrastination.

When you start a new task and you see the time you have allocated to yourself right away, the "pressure" will help you focus. If you're at a meeting or on a call, you can tell the other person in advance how much time you can dedicate to them, and use your watch/phone to track the time for yourself. If you work on a computer, again, there are many easy time-tracking apps available that will even notify you with a sound signal.

A list of tasks that includes time estimates provides support to your mind by giving it a clear order, so it doesn't get lost in many alternatives of what it should be focusing on at a given moment. What's more, when you make an educated guess of how much time each task on your daily list should take, you will see that when summed up, the final number is rarely as monstrous as you expect it to be. Only when we drift through our duties without much in-advance planning, various jobs end up needlessly stretched out. Or emails that could be dealt with within a few minutes take dozens more, as we simultaneously answer calls, check our social profiles, stare from the window, or dream about early retirement.

When you look over your little list of tasks (if it's not that little, keep reading) and see that altogether you've planned "only" a certain manageable number of hours for your most pressing responsibilities, you will start your day motivated rather than overwhelmed. You know that if you get them done (+) within a scheduled time estimate, there'll still be enough time left in your day to spend on other fun activities, family, friends, or taking care of yourself.

Don't aim for perfection. You're not a robot. The goal here is not to turn yourself into a soulless machine that walks through life ticking off tasks. The note-taking is but a simple, easy, and useful tool to become a friend of your time and achieve whatever you wish to achieve.

 Once the last one is completed, your stress level should diminish substantially. If you finish all the items, in both the essential and important categories, you're a champion and you can go to bed pleased with yourself. Most probably you will even have some time left for the optional and other pleasurable items.

Imagine having this feeling of satisfaction 365 times in a year. Imagine going to bed each night knowing that there are more than enough hours in your day.

The key rules to follow:

a) Don't get "greedy"

The further in your career, the more confident you become in terms of how many tasks you can tick off your list at once, how many meetings you can squeeze into a single day, or how many emails you can reply to within an hour. Yet, some tasks always slip through the cracks, people grow frustrated because you don't find enough time to talk to them, or trivial emails eat up too big a chunk of your mornings.

This is an absolutely normal thing to happen, but if you aspire to retain at least a modest sense of "having control," you need to HELP YOUR MIND WELL IN ADVANCE by pointing to the things that are genuinely important. When your brain is presented with a large array of alternatives at a given moment, and the criteria for decision-making are not clear, it will most probably opt for the easiest option, or a random one, not the most relevant, or the most efficient.

When you have a small set of the most critical tasks laid out for the day, your decisions on how to deal with your time yield better results. You would still need to fight off the beast of procrastination. And you would be ambushed by unexpected urgencies or crises that cannot wait to steal your attention. But when that happens, you have something at hand to refer to, even if it means reshuffling your priorities.

> **Even in critical situations, a person can take a deep breath and make a quick mental evaluation of what is and what is not truly urgent.**

It's not hard to draw an endless list of tasks we would like to get done. Every day, we take part in the race that never stops. There is no limit to what one can do, or should do.

But remember: there is a limit to your day, and there is a limit to your life. Night falls to remind us that one big bite of our time is gone. And when all is said and done, the dark will stay just as our time will be gone altogether.

So make your days worthwhile by making your own decisions as to what you truly care about.

b) Learn what is or isn't important

At first, it may not be easy to decide which task is essential and which one is "just important," let alone simply optional. We do become more experienced over time in prioritizing, but it's the nature of life to challenge us with situations and obstacles we fail to account for.

As mentioned above, the lists of tasks we can set up for ourselves are in theory endless. If we're to decide every single day which ones to focus on and which ones to ignore, it's helpful to be aware of OUR GENERAL GOALS, for a month, a quarter, a year, or a lifetime. Otherwise, there's a chance that we will be constantly frustrated no matter how hard we try.

Isn't a task the same thing as a goal?

No.

A goal is a final destination. A task is one step forward.

Let's look at the very beginning of each year.

For some people, it's the (only) day when they become motivated to lay out new goals for themselves. Some others would tell you that New Year's resolutions are just plain silly. No one really follows them through, do they?

What happens, in reality, is that a person lands their eyes on an ambitious goal, but at

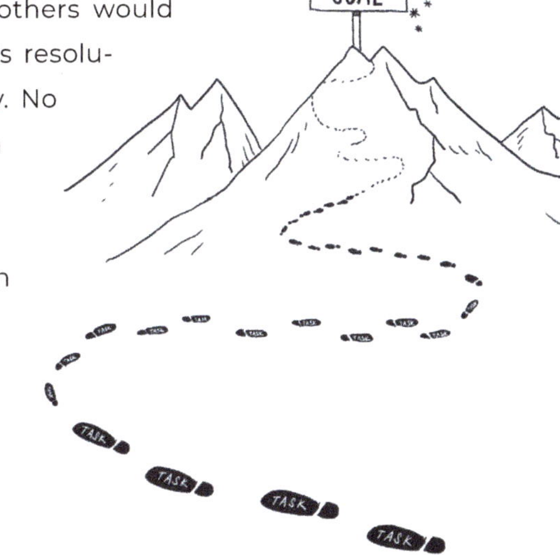

the same time they forget to draw up a clear roadmap that may lead them to it. Then, within a few weeks, they get discouraged since nothing major seems to have changed.

Their expectations were too high. The circumstances were not favorable. Someone else sabotaged their efforts… By the middle of the year, they don't even remember that they ever wanted to change anything in the first place. Or they do, but they choose to hush that memory to avoid the unpleasant taste of failure.

Likewise, in everyday life, a lot of people don't believe anything significant will ever happen to them, whether we talk about their private or professional domain. Now and then, they wish for something more appealing; they may even take a few random steps forward, but they eventually give up, convinced that dreams are for dreamers.

Others, on the contrary, settle on a straightforward road of working hard and doing what is expected of them, "believing," or rather "hoping," that there must be a reward for all that toil somewhere further down the road. Or they drift along, instead, arbitrarily or opportunistically clinging to anything that temporarily offers a prospect of a better future.

Such people refuse to make a decision for themselves and answer the question of WHAT EXACTLY IT IS THEY WANT TO FIND AT THE END OF THE JOURNEY.

Doing so would mean taking full responsibility of what needs to be done, which is tough, uncomfortable, and risky, since one cannot blame anyone else for their potential defeats.

A popular quote says, "Genius is 1% talent and 99% hard work."

Do we need to be endowed with special skills to succeed as entrepreneurs or shall we rather stop offering ourselves empty excuses and learn how to prioritize and organize our time?

Decide what goals you want to pursue this month/quarter/year, so that, when a task comes up, it's easy for you to designate its significance and urgency. The key to efficient time management is not to leave such decisions to the very last minute. At first, before you find and become comfortable with your own system, they might come off as micro-managing. But once you get the hang of these principles, they will merge seamlessly into each of your days, just as brushing your teeth has.

Unexpected events arise all the time, but when you are always aware of your current goals, you react fast, while staying flexible and at peace with the time you have.

2 – Focus

Procrastination is a sneaky witch who seldom rests. She is waiting day and night for any brief moment when we lower the guards of our attention so she can lure us away from what is truly important.

She is hard to beat. She wears many faces, and she metamorphoses faster than we could ever imagine. She knows our weakest points, our lowest desires, our deepest fears. She feeds on stealing away our precious time. She laughs when she catches us throwing it around as if there were no end to it.

Focus is a rare skill to see, especially now in the 21st century. Every second, we are showered with new information, new content, new ways of entertainment. We have much more choice in terms of how to deal with our time, even though the more we have, the less satisfied we feel. Having too many alternatives to grab leaves us anxious about possibly missing something "just a bit better."

The lack of focus plagues the character of every unhappy, unfulfilled, and unsuccessful individual.

The skill of focus and concentration is not only important for succeeding at work. It goes far beyond that. It's paramount for achieving our most ambitious dreams and for unlocking our full potential.

Imagine that your mental abilities were transformed into a bow, and your practical skills you use to build, create, and lead into a set of arrows. Imagine standing in front of a row of round targets.

You're calm, fast, precise. You know your weapon's strengths and weaknesses. And that's why you score a good number of points, maybe even hit the black center, straight away.

But there is a catch. With every target you hit, three others appear in its place.

No problem! You think you can still succeed as long as you hit as many of them as possible.

What if you knew that some of those targets were real and some faux? What if you could learn to tell them apart? Then perhaps, regardless of how many of them surrounded you, you could use your arrows wisely, and you could finish off within a fraction of the time you would otherwise need.

On one hand, the ability to focus is affected by quite a few bodily factors: the quality of our sleep, food, our emotional state… notably by OUR OVERALL ENERGY LEVEL. On the other hand, FOCUS IS A STATE OF MIND: a mental commitment to filter out useless and redundant thoughts.

These two are closely related. The capacity to succeed in practically anything starts and ends with the amount of inner energy we are capable of accumulating. If we struggle with procrastination and a lack of focus, the first step would be to look at the *"golden" five*: 1) how we breathe, 2) the quality of our sleep, 3) the quality of the food we eat, 4) how well hydrated we are, and 5) the physical fitness activities we do. The better we are at all of them, the higher our mental clarity.

The second step would be a diligent selection of the targets to aim at.

A surprisingly high number of people have only a vague idea, at any random moment you'd care to ask, as to what the major goals they wish to pursue in their lives are.

A clear set of goals that we actually care about gives our mind an explicit and understandable order. A roadmap to follow, so we don't get lost. A strong reference for our daily decision-making.

Besides, a crystal clear focus on what we want inevitably attracts the RIGHT OPPORTUNITIES. Better, worthier targets.

The moment we focus our sights on what the purpose of our efforts is, the fog that has made our personal and professional journey difficult to follow starts lifting up.

A targeted mental focus on a specific task is crucial to get the work done. Faster, better, ready to move on. Also, an unabridged focus on a person we're talking to is vital for creating a deeper connection, improving our mutual communication, and DEVELOPING MEANINGFUL RELATIONSHIPS, BOTH PERSONAL AND PROFESSIONAL.

Just try it for yourself. It sounds obvious, even banal, but just try for once to give full attention to the next person you meet. Focus on their words and register the true meaning behind them. Look into their eyes. Observe their body language. Listen.

At first, it may seem to be an unnecessary time waster. You're too busy for this! And does it even make a difference?

It does. It makes all the difference in the world because the levels of trust and engagement increase dramatically when you offer your full focus to the other person.

Remember all those missed opportunities, broken relationships, delayed projects... as a result of needless miscommunications?

Or think about your professional network, your support net. The stronger its threads, the higher the chances of you succeeding.

It's not always fun: doing what we care about. And if the road to what we want, or need, to get done is outright painful, our mind will inherently navigate towards something rather more enjoyable, more gratifying. The response to that is: Clarity. Energy. Practice. Make sure you remind yourself of your goals. Learn how to recharge yourself. Keep trying.

BUSYNESS

When a colleague or a friend of yours tells you "I'm busy!," how do you feel? Do you feel sorry for them? Do you offer an appreciative look? Do you admire their hectic lifestyle? Are you envious of how much they manage to fit into their schedules?

The reality of the present day is that when we hear the expression "I'm busy," we mostly don't feel anything. People utter these words day in day out, as if being "unbusy" or (heaven forbid) occupied with just one activity at a time was a crime.

The human need to feel important, significant, noticed is too strong to be ignored. By saying that we're busy, we may be sending one of the following messages:

I'm needed.

I deserve respect.

I want you to pity me.

I want you to envy me.

(Or simply: YOU are not important to me right now.)

Obviously, it's natural that we feel overwhelmed at times with all the duties that fill our days. Especially when we run a business. Especially if we've not yet mastered the skill of managing our time.

However, the fact that there's a lot on our plate doesn't automatically preclude us from having control. Which is exactly what "being busy" means: not having control.

Or alternatively:

I'M BUSY. = I'VE NOT (YET) SUCCEEDED IN ORGANIZING MY TIME.

Is this the message you wish to convey? Is this the image you would like to build?

Efficient time management is not something that can be adopted overnight. It requires a good dose of experimenting, discipline, habit-building, and constant practice.

While you can find a lot of materials to learn from, you will inevitably end up developing your own system that works just for you. In the meantime, does everyone need to know that you're still at the very beginning of your journey?

Does your mind need to be constantly reminded that it has been failing?

So help yourself by banning this expression from your vocabulary. Imagine that the phrase "I'm busy" is so cliché and vulgar that you would feel ashamed once caught saying it.

How would it sound if you replaced "I'm busy" with:

My work involves quite a lot of responsibilities.

I'm (lucky to be) involved in a few engaging projects right now.

At the moment, I'm discovering which goals to focus on.

… and so forth?

Very often our own words have direct impact on our internal canvases or shape our beliefs in ways that become difficult to break later on.

Busyness is a restraint we place on ourselves to stay on the safe side. We feel occupied and needed without the painful necessity to make hard choices and focus on what is truly important. At the same time, it's a handy shield against the demanding expectations that have been placed on us by others.

Neutral or positive affirmations of being in control of our time relieve the tension that won't otherwise go away when there's a lot to do. What's more, a self-assured attitude makes us exude an aura of confidence and competency to the outer world.

HABITS

A habit is something you do regularly. It is a recurrent behavior you may or may not be aware of.

Bad habits might be at the core of your inability to control your time. Good habits, on the other hand, can help you resume this very same control.

Conscious development of a new habit follows the straightforward pattern of "DRAP":
A) DECIDE
B) REPLACE
C) ACTIVATE
D) PRACTICE

A) DECIDE

At the origin of every new habit is a DECISION TO ADOPT A NEW BEHAVIOR or a new way of thinking.

We may decide to lose weight because we wish to look prettier, or because we are trying to avoid health problems. We may decide to go to bed early because we want to be focused at work, or because we need an extra hour in the morning to schedule a sports activity. We may decide to break the habit of interrupting people when they talk because we would like to become more likable, or because we have resolved to polish our communication skills within a career transition.

The common reason why many people fail, though, is that they stop right here. Something has stimulated or motivated them to change their behavioral patterns, yet they jump directly to their application without fortifying their internal beliefs.

It's much easier to adopt a new behavior when it falls under the PRINCIPAL GOALS you've committed to set for yourself and pursue in a specific life period. However, your efforts to change yourself on the outside may prove to be tough, not because of your lack of discipline but because this new habit you hope to develop faces resistance of your core:

BELIEFS
VALUES
NEEDS

If we aspire to change our behavior on the outside, we first need to change our perception on the inside.

Take, for example, a person whose goal it is to write a book. For this to happen, she decides to wake up at 5 a.m. so she can write for two hours before going to work. But then, even though she makes a few attempts at getting out of bed early, within the first month, she comes to a conclusion that she's simply not disciplined enough, and eventually gives up.

What could have happened here was that her resolution was weaker than her routine of sleeping long. The resistance she faced when trying to embrace her new writing practice might have been driven by:

Belief: A person should not force herself to do anything that is uncomfortable.

Value: Health is the most important thing, and sleeping helps a person stay healthy.

Need: Sleeping brings so much pleasure.

All in all, her mind marked those two extra hours spent sleeping as PLEASURE, while waking up early as PAIN.

B) REPLACE

When we resolve to change our old ways of behaving or our old ways of thinking, first we need to either modify our core beliefs or adapt the new habit to them. If our old habits are derived from our common needs, we also need to look at new ways of satisfying these needs in a better (healthier, more efficient…) way.

> If a certain behavior is in accordance with our beliefs, needs, and values, we tend to associate it with pleasure.
>
> If it contradicts our beliefs, needs, and values, we tend to associate it with pain.

To get rid of an old habit, you need to identify the reasons why it creates pain for you. "It's not good for me" is not sufficient. Such a statement is based on an "external" reason to change your behavior: Someone told you… they say… you've read about… if you don't do it, you will have to deal with…

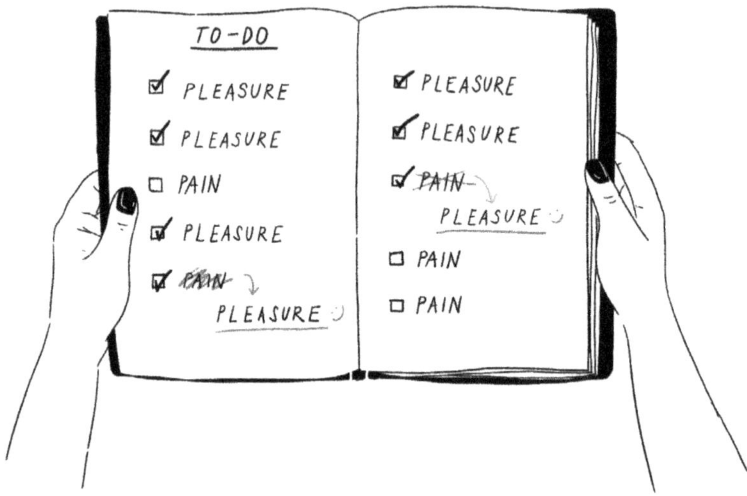

External pressure could, in theory, be strong enough for you to change your behavior, but most likely only temporarily. On top of that, it could cause a good dose of stress in your life if it denies your internal conviction.

Let's take a man who wishes to stop eating chocolate as another example. Chocolate obviously gives him a lot of pleasure, and because of his habit of gobbling up a few bars per day, he has gained plenty of unwanted weight.

Since his family and his friends have all noticed the new reality of his body shape, they keep throwing quite unpleasant comments at him. That's why one day he decides to replace chocolate with vegetables, which he has been otherwise avoiding like the plague since he was a small boy.

He is firmly determined to improve his eating habits. He has even made a plan on how much he aims to lose by the end of each week. Unfortunately, in his mind, chocolate still means pleasure, and eating vegetables a nuisance.

How much time do you think he has before giving up?

Replacing pleasure with pain is not the very best strategy for building new habits. On the contrary, replacing pleasure with another (possibly greater) pleasure, or even pain with pleasure, is much more efficient.

Imagine that the man from our example found a way to satisfy his needs in a healthier way while retaining the same amount of pleasure. Even better, that he changed his beliefs to the extent that his mind associated eating too much chocolate with pain.

Maybe it sounds a bit far-fetched to you at first, but just look at the people who have been successfully maintaining healthy eating habits for years. They may still enjoy eating chocolate, ice cream, or fries here and there, yet their fundamental belief is that such food harms their bodies. That's why eating junk food is only a temporary behavior in their case. It doesn't unwillingly develop into a new (undesired) habit since it contradicts what they believe in (junk food makes our body and mind suffer), need (good quality of life), and value (good health).

If we followed the same logic, we could see that some other people never develop a new (desired) habit of eating healthy as it contradicts what they believe in (I deserve to treat myself), need (emotional comfort), or value (freedom to do whatever I want).

C) ACTIVATE

Most habits are triggered by:

PLACE	➡	My behavior changes when I'm at a specific location.
TIME	➡	I behave in a certain way at a certain time (of the day, of the month, etc.).
PERSON	➡	When I meet/see/talk to person X, I behave in a certain way.
FEELING	➡	When I feel X [good/bad/stressed/sad/under pressure...], I behave in a certain way.
EVENT	➡	When X happens, I behave in a certain way.

The first step towards adopting a new habit is to identify the kind of behavior we want to replace. The second step is to transform our thinking to the point that our mind associates the old behavior with pain and the new behavior with pleasure. And the third step, just before we start putting the new habit into action, is to diagnose the relevant trigger.

Again, we aim at facilitating the whole process for ourselves well in advance. If we draw up the whole roadmap for our new behavior, our brain knows exactly what the instructions to follow are, when the time comes.

In a way, we reprogram ourselves.

Unfortunately, reprogramming a human mind is not as straightforward as reprogramming an operational system of a computer. The human mind is still much more complex, and it exhibits a significant resistance when we endeavor to do so.

Knowledge ≠ Belief: It's worth noting that just because you are aware of the undesirable consequences of your behavior, it won't be any easier for you to get rid of it. Smokers usually know very well what happens to their lungs and what the health risks related to their bad habit are, and still it doesn't make them stop. In many countries, tobacco companies are obliged to display unsettling graphic images on cigarette packs to make smokers quit, but very few do so despite being exposed to them. Why?

Not only might such warnings be perceived as external manipulation, which we innately detest, they also produce an "I must" instead of "I want" assessment in our head. These two are close to each other since we habitually push ourselves to improve based on what we know is best for us. So both the "information" and the "motivation" are present, and yet we often fail at replacing an old habit with a new one.

A sufficient amount of high-quality and thought-provoking information is an important factor in reprogramming our mind and changing our beliefs. However, firstly, such information should not be forced on us. We're always more prone to trust things we come up with ourselves. Secondly, it should stimulate some "real" emotions.

But careful here: sometimes we feel bad just because we hate or pity ourselves for failing. Even though self-hate can to a certain extent be a motivator to move forward, it's not the healthiest one.

If we go back to smokers... Regardless of what they know, smoking gives them pleasure. In their mind, the habit of pulling out a cigarette can be associated with a private moment, a moment of relaxation, for example, which is reinforced by the addictive nature of nicotine.

When they smoke, they feel good (mental addiction). When they don't, they get irritated and nervous (physical addiction). Pleasure versus pain.

In conclusion, self-education and information alone won't make you change your behavior unless you employ it to turn pleasure into pain or vice versa.

D) PRACTICE

As soon as we've given fresh orders to our mind, we should start putting our new habit into practice.

 Hence, it's more efficient to start with smaller steps and weaken the resistance gradually.

For example, instead of reducing our daily working hours from sixteen to eight right away, the better objective may be to lower the workload by one hour at first, until the new behavior is settled. Then we can follow up the same road and keep raising the bar steadily.

Besides, it's important to have a specific plan of what the old behavior will be replaced with. For example, if I aim to work an hour less on a given day, what am I going to use this hour for?

Following the same logic, if we wish to improve our communication skills, it's better to test the new behavior on a specific person, or on a group of people at a specific location. This also offers space for experimenting and modification of our behavioral roadmap if we find out that our original assumptions were not correct.

It's worth noting that as far as habit-building goes, temporary failure is rather normal, and it's nothing to be demotivated by. If we fail at developing a new habit, despite regular practice, it simply means that we've not worked deep enough on formulating and fortifying new beliefs, or on adjusting our behavior to our core values.

First and foremost, transforming our behavioral patterns and forming new habits is a process. An individual process. No matter what anyone tells you, you know yourself best. You know your story best. You know the canvas of your mind best. Only you can find the ways out and in.

DECIDE

1. Make sure the new way of behaving or thinking falls under your current life goals.

2. Establish that your new behavior is in line with your:

Beliefs
Needs
Values

If yes, move to the next point. If it's not in line with your:

Beliefs – To begin with, consider modifying your new habit in a way that it does conform to what you believe in. Or change your beliefs, if you can. Write them down and find ways how to rewire your mind.

Need – Modify your new behavior in order to keep your needs satisfied or find other means of satisfying them.

Value – Our values don't change overnight, since they represent beliefs and concepts that are really important to us, and being aware of them helps us explain the bigger picture of our behavior.

Values are closely linked to our beliefs, but not every belief develops into a value.

If your new habit contradicts your core values, there's little chance that you're going to succeed.

If you come to the realization that some of your values hold you back, ask yourself a few questions: Are they old or relatively recent? How did they appear in my life? Who or what influenced me? How do they reflect in my choices, my decisions, my actions?

EXAMPLE: I would like to develop a new habit of mapping out my tasks for the next day before I go to bed.

DOES THIS HABIT FALL UNDER MY CURRENT GOALS?

Yes. Better time management will help me improve my productivity at work (goal 1) and spend more time with my family (goal 2).

IS IT IN LINE WITH MY BELIEFS/NEEDS/VALUES?

At first, most of us would say "yes" at this point, since we've just plucked up the courage to improve ourselves. Yet, it's crucial to dig deeper and investigate what has been stopping us so far.

Then we may come up with something like:

In the evening, I'm tired, and I prefer activities that relax me (need). Planning my duties for the next day is stressful (belief). On the other hand, I would really like to schedule my tasks in a more efficient way, so I can spend more quality time with my family (value).

We can see that in this case, the key to succeeding is to change our belief that task planning is stressful.

Rewiring our mind

It's necessary to transform the perception TASK MANAGEMENT = STRESS to TASK MANAGEMENT = RELIEF.

Possible ways:

➡ Set a specific time and a method for planning your tasks. Regular practice leads to confidence, which results in reduced level of stress.

➡ Write down all the benefits of daily task management. Spend a few minutes over each one of them, while your mind is pushed to associate scheduling with pleasure, not pain. If necessary, repeat.

➡ Think about how your new habit will have a positive impact on others. Stay specific in your deliberations. Imagine the people you care about and how their life may change as a result of your new behavior.

➡ Link your new habit to an activity that is already pleasurable. For example, if you like to watch your favorite TV show in the evening to "relax," make a deal with yourself that you will start with a 20-minute session of planning your next day before you put the show on. Then, not only will you find comfort in the show itself but also in the fact you've put the duties of the next day "on paper." Clear mind, pleasure increased.

REPLACE

You've just decided to say "yes" to a new habit, which means you would need to say "no" to some of the old ones.

If you're saying YES to this, what do you need to say NO to instead?

There's almost always something you have been doing until this moment as a close alternative, even though at first it may seem that the two behaviors are not related.

What would I do if I didn't do this?

How would it make me feel?

What impact would my old behavior have on others?

I could set aside some time to plan my tasks for the next day when the children are already asleep in their beds. But even though it's something I would like to learn to do, when the day is almost over, I usually avoid thinking about work and try to relax myself by having a good drink and watching some good TV.

I must say... I don't feel guilty, only a little, since my need to cool off is much stronger at such moments. On the following mornings, on the other hand, I get buried with emails, meetings, and unexpected calls... scolding myself for not having prepared my day. The frustration culminates in the evening... when I numb myself with TV, food, and alcohol.

Such a pattern of behavior has an impact on both my colleagues at work and on my family. I stress myself even before reaching the office, being preemptively on alert and worried by "what the day may bring."

I guess, deep inside, I start every day expecting failure.

Then at work, I act less than "diplomatic." I have difficulties focusing, and I tend to blame others if things are not going as I would expect them to.

As far as my family goes, there are only few days in a month when I come back home early enough to spend the whole evening with my partner and my children. Most often, I excuse myself by pointing to my job being too demanding and to my drive to excel at it. To some extent it works, since I get a decent salary; however, I sense that we grow more distant. Besides, I do everything only for them, so what's the point of all this if we stop communicating with each other?

YES: I will spend 20 minutes every evening prioritizing and scheduling tasks for the next day.

NO: I will spend 20 minutes less in front of the TV.

– I will have 20 minutes less pleasure (switching off my brain and passively watching something entertaining).

+ I will start my days with less stress.

+ Due to the lower amount of stress, I'll get better at communicating with my teammates.

+ I will know when to stop, which will allow me to go back home earlier.

+ I will spend considerably more time with my family.

ACTIVATE

Identify a specific trigger of your old/new behavior.

EXAMPLE: When it's time to work on my plan for the next day, I'm usually too tired to follow through.

PLACE: home (comfort zone)

TIME: evening (quieter and calmer)

PERSON: x

FEELING: exhaustion

EVENT: when children have gone to bed (possibly)

When we are not able to change the triggers, at least not immediately (for example, the feeling of tiredness makes us fail at scheduling our work tasks), we need to find a way around.

EXAMPLE: Could I find an alternative time, somewhere after I finish my daily work and before going to bed, when I still retain a reasonable amount of energy? Maybe right after dinner... after having a shower?

Then the new trigger might look like this:

When I come home (time/place/event), I will have a quick shower and eat something together with my family. Being refreshed (feeling), I will sit for 20 minutes to plan my tasks for the next day. Like that, I will clear my mind to fully focus on my leisure and family time.

PRACTICE

At this point, we have everything we need: a specific road-map to changing our old (undesirable) behavior and adopting a new (desirable) one.

The purpose of daily practice is not only to strengthen the link between the new habit and our needs, beliefs, and values. We should use it also for exploring ourselves, experimenting, and modifying the original roadmap.

It's not wrong to miss the target the very first time. The mind of a human being is a beautiful and sophisticated system, which can both help us achieve anything we want, if used correctly, or hold us back, without us even noticing.

You will always face some resistance, that's why you need to keep learning and discovering how your mind works, so it cannot trick you into giving up.

Start with small, modest changes. See how they affect you. If there's no resistance left, move forward, until you are comfortable with your new habit and your mind accepts it as something that is wanted and agreeable.

80/20 PRINCIPLE

The 80/20 rule, or the Pareto principle (named after Italian economist Vilfredo Pareto), says that roughly 80% of the outcomes come from roughly 20% of the inputs. For example, 20% of your employees are responsible for 80% of the sales results. Or, 20% of your customers bring about 80% of the total revenue.

The principle is just an estimate of a typical distribution; however, it helps us understand the common phenomenon we can observe in our daily lives: some resources and activities contribute to the targets we aim at significantly more than others.

As to time management, let's consider the fact that the MAJORITY OF OUR RESULTS COME FROM THE MINORITY OF OUR ACTIONS. Once we identify the right activities to focus on, we can ditch the "80%" (or at least part of them) of those that are "eating up" our time and at the same time bringing about only a fraction of our desired goals.

For entrepreneurs, in general, it's tough to embrace a thought that ONE COULD DO MORE WITH LESS. Most of us hold a view that 24 hours in a day are not enough. As if we were being deprived of something we are entitled to.

I want to achieve so much, but I have so little time!

Many would be surprised that the Earth has little in the way of intentions to stop revolving around the sun, just because we have made up our mind to go into business. And definitely not because we fail to appreciate and make good use of the time we have.

Since we were born, day and night have been taking their turns with absolute certainty. Still, we often find ourselves shocked and off guard when the day starts fading away.

No! Not yet. I've still got so much on my plate!

Would you treat money like you treat your days? Imagine that someone made you this proposal: "I will give you a large sack of golden coins, but I'm not going to tell you how much there is for you in total. Every day, you will simply receive 24 coins, until there's nothing left."

There may be people among us who would simply spend everything and wait for the next day to replenish their pockets. But those aren't people we typically call "entrepreneurs." People who are considerate about managing their resources would rather use some of the coins on the necessary or wanted expenses and save the rest for future use.

You may object that we cannot save hours for future use. Can't we?

Isn't an hour spent on learning an investment into our future? What about an hour spent on teaching someone else something new? Sharing with and listening to our colleagues, our employees, our partners, our friends, our children?

> **An hour passed is an hour lost. An hour lived is an hour preserved.**

If we go back, the 80/20 rule tells us that only around an hour and a half of an 8-hour working day, or two and a half hours of a 12-hour working day, for instance, yield the majority of the desired outcomes. For an archetypal entrepreneur who aims at working as many hours as possible, this might be hard to swallow. In fact, it's easier for them to run the strategy of aiming for the best and trying the hardest they can than admitting to themselves that too many of the activities they pursue on a daily basis bring only little, both to their businesses and to their lives.

In conclusion, your time management skills will significantly improve from the very moment you start putting the statement "the majority of the results proceed from the minority of my actions" into practice. You can immediately free yourself of many "unyielding" activities and gain extra hours in your days for those that really matter.

An hour passed
is an hour lost.
An hour lived
is an hour
preserved.

FREE TIME

We define free time, or leisure time, as the time we spend on activities outside our main work duties. Although some people love their work, and they enjoy every minute of it, even for them it usually doesn't fill 100% of their days.

Our free time should in ideal case serve to recharge our:

BODIES ➡ sleep, physical exercise, eating and drinking (not necessarily alcoholic beverages), sex...

and

MINDS ➡ creative and fun activities, learning, nurturing relationships, socializing, meditation...

Many entrepreneurs hold a firm opinion that leisure time is an extravagance they can't afford. The more hours they spend on growing their businesses, the higher chances of them succeeding. This is unfortunately as absurd as if we believed that stopping at a gas station to refuel our car is a luxury holding us back from getting to our destination as fast as possible.

If you are a car owner, it's absolutely natural for you to schedule regular refueling and maintenance stops in order to maintain the good performance of your transportation tool. If you are an entrepreneur, there's a chance that you suck at scheduling time for yourself, which would allow you to replenish your energy reserves so that you could continue on your journey strong and at full speed.

Eating more food is not enough.

Eating the right quantities of the right food at the right time is much better. Besides, we need to pay attention to regular intake of fluids, to replace the substantial amounts of water our body loses every day. When we take in less liquid than what we lose (perspiration, excretion, breathing, etc.), we become dehydrated. Dehydration has many harmful effects, such as tiredness, dizziness, and lethargy, but all in all, it's again tightly linked to energy deprivation.

Furthermore, before both eating and drinking, there is good quality sleep. This is when your body, including your brain, heals and repairs itself. You can function even with limited or poor-quality sleep, but, in the long-term, your health, productivity, focus, learning abilities, decision-making, communication, and sound eating habits get severely affected.

Why do we speak about such basic things such as sleeping and eating? Isn't free time mostly about having fun?

Undoubtedly, yes. Having fun is important, but it sits on the top of the pyramid. If we lack energy, we should use the "free" time we have on servicing our main working instrument, our body.

Many entrepreneurs start focusing on improving their minds before improving their bodies. They look for ways to perform better, concentrate better. They meditate or even pray. They try hard to learn new skills. They consume loads of new information. All this on less than ideal levels of internal energy.

Sharpening our minds starts with recovering our bodies. When our breathing, sleeping, eating, drinking, and overall fitness habits are helping us stay strong and full of energy, the second step is to work on containing the thoughts that limit our progress and drain us second by second.

Every "negative" (harmful, unproductive…) thought is a huge energy killer. Thousands of such thoughts are drifting back and forth through our minds at any given moment, and it's solely up to us which we choose to materialize by concentrating our attention on them, i.e., injecting them with our spare energy and growing them from an ephemera to a permanent parasite.

Time off is important for any worker, but for entrepreneurs twice as much. They strive to create solutions for seemingly unsolvable problems. They spend years building their visions with little or no guarantee of success. They face rejection and resistance, sometimes even suspicion and mockery. They are inclined to invest all their personal resources—energy, skills, knowledge, time, money, relationships—into something only they alone believe in. They're leaders, innovators, makers. They are called crazy, fools, and children who forgot to grow up. They need to be relentless in pursuing their vision, yet bright enough to embrace compromise. They're walkers in the dark forest, depending on the compass in their heart to bring them to the right destination.

Good entrepreneurs give ear to the needs of the people they serve: their customers. Successful entrepreneurs realize that their own needs are equally important, so they can serve well and long while avoiding physical and mental burnout.

Every day has just 24 hours, and we carve out a major part of it for work. Unfortunately, too often, we use the remaining hours on generating extra (avoidable) stress.

It is a sad paradox of our lives that we seem to favor unhappiness over happiness. We grow and cultivate negative thoughts. We dwell in the past, or fear the future, instead of focusing on the good in the present moment. We're never satisfied.

In fact, we believe that happiness and satisfaction are something that should arrive automatically as a reward for our efforts. We refuse to take responsibility for our own well-being. When we have an extra hour, rather than healing our minds and restoring our bodies, we switch ourselves into an inactive mode. Instead of attempting to fix and enrich our thinking, we simply resort to comforting our minds for the short-lived moment.

Passive entertainment is the first remedy most individuals are after when they feel overwhelmed and exhausted. It's fast, always available, and relatively cheap (thank you, the Internet), and efficient at numbing our feelings and suppressing the thoughts we seek to run away from. However, what passive entertainment cannot provide is supplying us with massive volumes of energy, which we need before anything else.

A thought is naught without the energy we invest in it.

We need energy to focus. We need energy to come up with new ideas. We need energy to create. We need energy to persevere.

An entrepreneur whose body and mind are not working well is like a driver whose car is broken. Good time management and productivity skills, therefore, don't only presume that a person is able to plan, schedule, and execute their daily tasks. It means that they acknowledge the importance of time dedicated to activities, moments, or people who help them accumulate extra energy, and they are capable of arranging their daily program accordingly.

32. The Boss in Charge

*I*f you're to succeed in life, you need two things: time and energy. When you have sufficient time and energy, you can achieve anything you want, provided that you channel them in the right direction.

TIME

We're in control of our time when we have learned how to value it.

We're in control of our time when we are able to recognize what is truly important.

We're in control of our time when we are capable of holding focus.

We're in control of our time when we know how to develop good habits.

We're in control of our time when we use it to generate ENERGY.

ENERGY

Successful entrepreneurs are passionate and dedicated self-learners with the goal of providing value for their customers, who use (and possibly pay for) their products and services. For them, achieving this level of success requires a constant supply of energy.

Problem-solving, creativity, intuition, tenacity, or continuous personal growth… they all call for massive quantities of energy.

So where to get it?

Scores of high-achieving individuals face excessive stress, anxiety, depression, insomnia, overweight, heart diseases, or accelerated aging, even though such grave physical and mental issues are not something that we would primarily associate with success as such.

Stress is a bodily reaction to a situation that, based on the evaluation of our mind, requires an extra amount of energy. Such expenditure can be beneficial if we're in true danger and we face the immediate need of a "fight or flight" response. When this occurs, our body is pumped with stress hormones, such as adrenaline, our pulse and breathing rate increase, pupils get dilated, and blood moves from our digestive system to our larger muscles. However, unless we fight for survival or flee from our enemies on an everyday basis, a similar physiological reaction is not desirable since it affects our overall health.

Unfortunately, our thoughts (those crafty saboteurs!) activate a stress response several times per day. When we open our email inbox. When we spot unpaid bills. When we receive an unexpected call from work. When we get into a petty fight with our partner. When we fear a looming deadline… Not only do we squander our energy, we may also develop chronic diseases as a result of our body being under constant strain.

We need energy to control our thoughts and feelings in stressful moments. We lose energy when we're stressed. Energy, energy, all over again.

The three pillars of generating and accumulating sufficient levels of energy are:

BODY
SOUL
PEOPLE

I. BODY

a) Breathing

b) Sleeping

c) Eating

d) Drinking

e) Moving

This is the first, foremost, and absolutely unavoidable step. When we sense that there's something wrong with us, our lives... with our thoughts, our feelings, our relationships... there is a good chance that fixing all the five areas above will improve the majority of the issues we struggle with.

BREATH OF LIFE

The right breathing technique infuses our blood with oxygen and simultaneously calms and energizes our body and soul. Chronic stress, on the other hand, causes our breath to become shallower, which can result in fatigue, dizziness, anxiety, or muscle tension.

The correct breathing is slow, steady, and relaxed. When we breathe in the right way, we engage diaphragm, a dome-shaped sheet of muscle that separates the abdominal cavity (our belly) from the thoracic cavity (our chest), and the proper exchange of gases is activated: oxygen in / carbon dioxide out. When we inhale, our diaphragm contracts to help us get as much air into our lungs as possible (the volume of the thoracic cavity increases); when we exhale, the diaphragm relaxes (the volume of the thoracic cavity decreases) to help us expel all of the air.

· CALM BREATHING = CALM MIND

When we are under stress, we take rapid, small, shallow breaths, engaging chest muscles rather than the diaphragm, to inflate the lungs. You may notice that shoulders of people who are upset typically move up and down, together with their rib cage, as they take in fast, short breaths.

Chest breathing causes too much carbon dioxide to be flushed out of the blood. As oxygen and carbon dioxide are bound to each other, the low levels of carbon dioxide lead to the oxygen/carbon dioxide balance being shifted and to decreased levels of oxygen supply in the body's cells, including the vital organs, such as our heart and our brain.

Oxygen deficiency in our cells then badly affects our nervous system, which may, in the long term, contribute to faster aging and severe chronic diseases, including cancer.

As early as 1931, Otto Heinrich Warburg received a Nobel Prize for proving that while normal cells need oxygen for survival, cancer cells can live without it.

SWEET SLEEP

As much as we need proper breathing to keep our body alive, we need good quality sleep to help our body restore and heal itself. When we sleep, essential hormones are released to help the body develop and grow, our damaged cells are repaired, and our immune and cardiovascular systems are recharged. Besides, when we sleep, our brain consolidates and stores new information, creates links between memories, and prepares itself to soak up even more.

Good quality sleep is therefore not only important for our body to work well, but also for our mind to learn and stay creative.

In simple terms, the sleeping time is when our batteries get recharged. When you plug your phone into a charger, you know you need to wait for a while before the battery bars go up again. Analogically, we need a certain number of hours of deep, restorative sleep so that we can function to our full potential.

The exact amount of sleep people need varies with age, and it's up to you to find the right sleeping pattern. Pay attention to the days when you jump out of bed, motivated and full of energy. Maybe it's simply your lucky day, and maybe you've just gifted yourself with a night of deep healing and relaxation.

Dedicate some time to identifying an ideal right time for you to go to bed and the ideal amount of hours you need to feel that you are at your 100%.

Obviously, the overall quality of sleep is affected by many other factors too: stress levels and breathing (as seen above), proper hydration, and the quality of food. One cannot go without the other. However, although they are all equally important, sleep is the first area to look at when we are feeling exhausted and sinking into negative thoughts.

FUEL, NOT WASTE

We eat because we're hungry. We eat because it's fun. We eat because we're feeling down. We eat because we're angry. We eat because we're bored.

Strangely enough, it seems that we often consume food as a response to the dictate of our mind, rather than our body.

The body needs food as a source of energy and essential nutrients—carbohydrates, proteins, fats, vitamins, minerals, and water—that help it grow, heal, and perform its key duties. The part of our food that cannot be used is merely waste that leaves the body through the large intestine.

In general, we tend to overeat. Our body requires food to work and restore itself, yet in reality, it needs relatively little, compared to all the meals and snacks we are able to consume in a single day. Even people who aim at maintaining a healthy lifestyle often eat higher quantities of food than their bodies demand to perform the essential functions.

Food portions have gotten much bigger over the last decades. Fast food and pre-packed food have become a daily routine for most of us. The fast and tasty beats the slow and healthy. Just fill up the stomach and get a dose of fat and sugar for an instant bump of pleasure. And let's hope our body won't fail us once again, and that it will be able to suck in a few traces of vital nutrients from the junk we've just served it.

It's been considered a part of common knowledge for a while that the majority of chronic diseases are related not only to stress but also to our bad eating habits. Moreover, those two are married to each other.

Why is it that we turned something so fundamental and gratifying into another thing that is slowly killing us?

In numerous developed countries, food has become easy to obtain, at any time of the day. It's a quick, guaranteed, and relatively inexpensive way to comfort ourselves. Unfortunately, it's frequently the case that the poorer quality, the lower the price. In many places around the globe, high-quality, nutritious, or even organic food is a luxury which a lot of families cannot afford.

Sugar-based junk food, in particular, is quite cheap, and it comes in countless varieties. Besides that, even easier than munching on a sugary snack is drinking up our pleasure in the form of sweetened drinks. It enters our body practically immediately. When deprived of it, we become restless and tired. Liquid sugar has become a serious addiction of not only a large portion of our adult population but regrettably also of our children.

The human body is a beautiful, sophisticated system that knows exactly what to do and what it needs to carry us successfully through our lives. For the most part, it is even capable of getting along well despite our best efforts to vandalize it with the rubbish we push down our throats.

However, waste is still waste, and as long as there is too much of it coming in, the system, albeit highly advanced, starts breaking down slowly but surely.

Food can still bring pleasure, but we should never forget that it's a tool to live, above anything else. When we think of what to eat, we should make smart choices such as the ones we make, quite automatically, when we pick the right fuel for our car.

Try to imagine how difficult it must be for the body to be constantly cleaning itself from the excess waste. How much energy it takes to keep everything in motion.

It's important to realize that as long as the digestive system is constantly in harness, our body never rests to be able to heal itself.

1) **Moderate quantities of food**
2) **Food with high nutrient content**
3) **Longer pauses in between meals so the body can absorb the essential nutrients and get fully rid of the waste**

In plenty of cultures and religions, fasting is an important discipline, not only as a part of one's spiritual and self-discovery journey but because it's a traditional way to cleanse and rejuvenate the body.

For many people, the idea of "not eating" is quite terrifying, though. Even a mere one day of fasting is unimaginable for the individuals whose main source of pleasure in life is food. At the same time, when we are sick or tired, most of the time we don't need complex, artificial, and costly medications or treatments. We should simply leave our body to work and take care of itself instead of incessantly digesting.

If food is the main, or only, source of pleasure in your life, then you have a problem. The urge to eat more will always be hard to beat, as your mind will do everything in its power to trick you into not giving it up. Bear this in mind if you wish to lose weight or reduce your addiction to sugar, fat, or over-eating in general.

When we need to get rid of a habit that is linked to pleasure, we should replace it with behavior that equals or surpasses that same amount of pleasure. Even better, we should associate the former behavior with pain. So take the time to study up on what excessive food consumption truly does to your body.

DRINK UP

Has it ever happened to you that you woke up after eight or seven hours of sleep and still felt exhausted? Have you ever been overcome with negative thoughts in the middle of a day for no reason?

Feeling moody again? Suffering from an inexplicable headache?

The quick fix in such cases can be to drink up a glass or two of pure or mineral water.

Chronic dehydration is a more common problem than you think. We feel thirsty when we're already slightly dehydrated. Prolonged dehydration leads to a range of health issues, yet even mild dehydration can affect our mood and mental abilities.

Not only do we forget to hydrate ourselves sufficiently throughout the day, we tend to favor sweet, caffeinated, or carbonated drinks due to their better taste. Such beverages, however, often burden our digestive system. Also, the gas and sugar create a "false" sense of refreshment, so the overall intake of pure water may be lower. At the same time, these drinks stimulate our taste buds and, due to the fluctuation of blood sugar levels, they can make us consume more food.

Around 60% of our total body weight is made up of water, which plays many vital roles, such as removal of harmful organisms, substances, and chemicals through excretory and digestive system, regulation of body temperature, dissolution of nutrients so they can enter the body tissues, circulation and transport of nutrients, or protection of body organs and tissues. The overall volume of water in our body depends on our gender, age, body composition, body temperature, and our current medical condition. Furthermore, we increase the level of water in our body through drinking, eating, and metabolism of nutrients, the chemical process that converts food molecules—carbohydrates, proteins, and fats—into energy. On the other hand, we lose water in the form of urine, stool, sweat, and in the breath we exhale.

A modern busy lifestyle, bad eating habits, and the absence of healthy hydration habits make us lose more water than we can afford. When our water intake is not sufficient, our body becomes dehydrated. Dehydration can then be defined as an abnormal loss of water and vital electrolytes like sodium or potassium.

Apart from sodium and potassium, the other important electrolytes for us are calcium, chloride, magnesium, phosphate, and bicarbonate. They need to be kept in an even balance for our body to function properly.

In simple terms, electrolytes are minerals that can be dissolved in water to conduct electrical impulses within the body, which is important for activation of muscle and nerve cells. In even simpler terms, they help carry the signals to the correct destination.

They also help to control the fluid level within and around the cells, ensuring they don't shrink or swell too much. Especially sodium is crucial for maintaining the right amount of water in our body.

That is why sports drinks often include sodium and potassium salts, to compensate for the loss of these minerals through sweating. People who suffer from diarrhea or excessive vomiting also recover faster when given electrolyte drinks. If such individuals drink only large quantities of pure water, the signs of dehydration can get even worse, as the remaining electrolytes get further diluted.

When the sodium concentration in one's blood sinks too low, a person can experience severe symptoms, such as seizures or loss of consciousness, which may eventually lead to death. If you aren't an athlete or sick, a balanced diet or moderate amount of mineral water should cover your basic needs of electrolytes. For example, fresh fruits and vegetables are a great source.

The symptoms of dehydration can vary from dry mouth, higher body temperature, tiredness, worsened concentration and work performance, lethargy, irritability, and headache, to more severe ones such as hallucinations, nausea, dizziness, higher pulse rate, low blood pressure, dry skin, and a decreased level of urine and sweat.

Do you think it's just a bit unlikely for this to be your case?

You may have become aware of the dangers of dehydration during hot weather. Also, if you do sports on a regular basis, you have probably learned by now that you need to replenish your body with fluids and electrolytes to fully recover after your workout has finished.

But what about people who spend most of their days behind a computer or in air-conditioned offices? Well, they still sweat, breathe, and pee.

For many entrepreneurs, managers, or executives, it's tough to find time to eat at times, let alone to keep in mind drinking at regular intervals so that they get enough water into their system. What trouble! Yet, what a fundamental prerequisite of staying focused, energized, and productive.

MOVE TO LIVE

The common perception is that when we work out, we lose energy.

When you are exhausted and overwhelmed with stress and work duties, exercise is probably the last thing you want to do. You would excuse yourself from moving your body with something like this on your mind: "Not today. I'm just too tired."

While it is true that good quality sleep, nutritious food, and proper hydration are key to staving off serious exhaustion, our overall level of energy also depends on how often we dedicate time to physical activities.

Obviously, when we perform physical exercise, our energy expenditure rises. Such energy loss should be then compensated with adequate intake of wholesome food and drinks. However, at the same time, using energy for a regular physical activity can pay off in the form of increased levels of energy in the long run.

When you exercise, you grow stronger and more resistant. The cells in your body contain mitochondria, which, simply put, are components that act as small "power plants." Their job is to convert oxygen (did you remember to breathe properly?) and nutrients (what about the composition of your food?) into energy. The more you exercise, the more mitochondria—*energy factories*—your body produces.

Mitochondria are distributed in all the cells and tissues of your body, with the exception of red blood cells, which transport oxygen to the other cells but don't use it to generate energy themselves. Muscles contain the highest accumulation of mitochondria in the body, in order to provide large amounts of energy when we move and exercise.

When we train our muscles repeatedly, the mitochondrial content increases. It means that the ability of our muscles to turn nutrients into energy improves, even after we have stopped exercising.

On the contrary, a sedentary lifestyle, aging, and a lack of exercise lead to a decline in the mitochondria count in our body, which can harm or kill cells altogether. Quite an easy fix, even for elder individuals, is to walk and move more. The increased muscle contraction then serves as a signal for the cells to produce more mitochondria. Also, the higher demand for energy causes the muscle cells to improve their ability to produce energy in the expectations of future exercise.

In essence, THE MORE YOU EXERCISE, THE MORE YOUR BODY BECOMES EFFICIENT IN CREATING EXTRA ENERGY.

During your busy day, as little as a short walk can help you beat your work-related fatigue. Also, not only does regular exercise help you maintain your overall health by regulating your body weight and reducing the risk of serious illnesses, such as heart diseases, it also improves your mood and mental abilities.

Exercise increases your heart rate, which then pumps more oxygen into your brain. What's more, it also stimulates restoration and growth of new brain cells. If you thought that after reaching adulthood, your brain is not capable of producing new cells, you were wrong.

In adult people, neurogenesis—the ability of the brain to produce new neurons—exists, although it is restricted to only two areas: olfactory bulb and hippocampus. The new neurons created in the hippocampus are important for the process of learning and retaining memory. They also help reduce stress and improve your mood.

Besides, it's important to note that exercise isn't the only factor that affects the efficiency of neurogenesis. When you don't sleep enough, the ability of your brain to create new cells is impaired as well. Last but not least, unhealthy eating and drinking habits play their negative role too.

And while drinking alcohol does not "kill" your brain cells, as your parents may have tried to scare you into believing, excessive alcohol consumption does disrupt the formation of new cells in your brain.

In general, if you wish to promote your brain health, you should limit your consumption of meals rich in saturated fat (animal fat, palm and coconut oil) and completely avoid trans fat (common in most industrially processed foods: various snacks, fried food, fast food, baked food, such as biscuits and pastries).

Trans fat is the worst type of fat you can eat. It is produced when vegetable oils are partially hydrogenated, i.e., processed to acquire extra hydrogen atoms, to make them more solid. Like this, food manufacturers obtain "more saturated" fat, or trans fat, as a cheaper substitute for animal fat, such as butter, for example. Apart from the price, the purpose of hydrogenation is also to prolong the shelf life of food products.

Not only does trans fat lack any nutritional value, except for increasing our calorie intake, it directly harms our body by raising the level of LDL cholesterol and reducing the level of HDL cholesterol in our blood.

We do need cholesterol. It is a substance vital for the functioning of the human body. For example, cholesterol is needed to produce vitamin D in the skin following sun exposure. That's why most of the cholesterol in our system is made by our own liver, although some foods contain it as well.

Cholesterol is not soluble in water, therefore it needs to be carried through the blood by some sort of "transporters." These are either a low-density lipoprotein (LDL), which may deposit cholesterol in our arteries, or a high-density lipoprotein (HDL), which moves the cholesterol out of our arteries. When there's too much of LDL cholesterol built up in artery walls, the passage for the blood flow gets narrow.

Hardening and narrowing of your arteries as a result of such plaque can start as early as your childhood and can end up in a range of serious diseases. In case a clot is formed and sticks, we can even experience a heart attack or a stroke.

Trans fat, therefore, significantly increases the risks of developing diseases of heart and blood vessels. It is one of the most harmful things to eat.

Next time, when you go shopping, simply go for less processed foods, or look carefully for the word "hydrogenated" on the label. And when eating out, bear in mind that hydrogenated oils are still used in many kitchens as a low-cost alternative. Frying in butter, lard, or coconut oil is expensive, and vegetable oil turns rancid quickly when exposed to heat. Partially hydrogenated oil, on the other hand, is more heat stable, therefore it doesn't need to be replaced that often.

On a better note, the "good" unsaturated fats, especially those containing omega-3 fatty acids, which are found in tuna, salmon, sardines, walnuts, flaxseeds, chia seeds and others, are essential nutrients that benefit practically all bodily processes, including the ability of our body to create new brain cells.

FAT?

Yes.

It includes fatty acids, which are essential for our body functions and our life energy.

SATURATED FAT?

Less.

It contains lower amount of essential fatty acids.

UNSATURATED FAT?

More.

It contains higher amount of essential fatty acids.

Both are rich in calories so they can make us gain weight when we don't use the energy they provide. However, consumption of only saturated fats can make us eat more since they include lower quantities of essential fatty acids, which we need for our body and mind.

Another factor that encourages the formation of new brain cells, apart from regular exercise and consumption of nutritious food, is an overall dietary restriction, which you can achieve by reducing the number of calories you normally consume. In addition, some studies have shown recently that neurogenesis can be promoted by certain dietary substances, such as flavonoids, found in blueberries and cocoa, resveratrol, found in red wine, or curcumin, found in the turmeric spice.

All in all, **WHAT YOU EAT** and **HOW MUCH YOU MOVE** can have an effect on your mood, thinking, learning, and memory, as a result of the production of new brain cells.

GOOD DIET + GOOD FITNESS ➡ BETTER MENTAL HEALTH

In a nutshell, if we wish to have **control** over our lives and attain **success**, we need to learn how to manage our time and how to generate a **copious quantity of energy**. The first and foremost step to produce our energy is then through our own **body**:

BREATHE

Don't steal oxygen from your body cells.

Go for slow and steady, rather than fast and shallow.

Engage your diaphragm more, and your chest much less.

SLEEP

Sleep to let your body heal and restore itself.

Sleep to promote the formation of new brain cells.

Find the sleeping pattern that makes you feel at your 100%.

FOOD

Eat to please your body, not your mind.

Eat lower quantities and less often.

Treat yourself with food rich in vital nutrients.

DRINK

Drink more water than what you lose.

Remember that even mild dehydration can affect your mood and performance.

When dehydrated, drink water with sodium and potassium.

EXERCISE

Move to make your body efficient at producing energy.

Move to promote the formation of new brain cells.

Help your brain to make neurons:

More exercise

More sleep

More omega-3

Fewer calories

Less saturated fat and trans fat

Less alcohol

And as a bonus, you may supercharge your meals with blueberries, cocoa, turmeric, or a glass of red wine.

II. SOUL

Your mind and your emotions often seem "out of your control" simply because you don't have enough energy in your body.

Imagine your **body** to be soil and your **thoughts** to be plants that grow on it.

Plants thrive on soil that is tilled, watered, and nourished. The better the quality of the soil, the better the quality of the plants growing on it.

Some plants smell. This smell is our **emotions**.

Some plants bear fruits. These fruits are our **achievements**.

Our mind is a gardener who, at birth, was given a piece of land to fulfill its **purpose** of building a beautiful garden.

Most gardeners are too occupied with themselves. They keep sitting on the ground for days, with their head buried in their hands, pondering why nothing good and useful grows around them. Weed has taken over and it stinks. The flowers lack color, the fruit is sour!

For all that, such a gardener starts pitying himself. Why does he live on such a barren land?

If he looked up, he would see that up there, in the sky, there is a big bright sun shining down on him and his

garden. It rises every single day to offer its light to the plants to grow. It's the **spirit** that makes everything in the garden live and flourish.

But since our gardener always keeps his head down, he came to believe that he is alone and that his efforts are futile.

Some gardeners, on the other hand, are grateful for the sun to appear in the morning. They greet it as they walk into the garden to pull out weeds, to water the plants they love, and to give the soil the nourishment it deserves. They know that without the sun, their garden would be a cold, dark place where nothing grows. Its light is a part of everything that makes the garden alive.

However, they also know that it takes hard, daily work on their side to cultivate flowers whose pleasing scents they can smell and grow trees whose sweet fruit they can enjoy.

A body without soul and spirit is just a piece of flesh, much as a garden without plants and sun is just a piece of unproductive land. And much as we nourish the soil and cultivate the plants that grow on it, we need to take care of our body and pick which thoughts to cultivate and which ones to weed out.

Our mind is the gardener who is capable of making such a decision. Yet, it can't plant good thoughts and pick out bad ones if the body is neglected.

When we, with the help of our body, create enough energy, we have the power to instill order into our mind. Bad thoughts take up a large portion of our daily energy expenditure. It is them behind all the stress we experience, not people, or our work. They are behind the feelings of frustration, anger, anxiety, or loneliness, not what others tell us or what happens to us.

Thoughts pass through our heads day and night, back and forth... both good and bad. There's no need to blame ourselves for a certain thought coming to our mind. It's the nature of thoughts. They simply exist. But we can blame only ourselves when we give attention to a potentially harmful thought and dedicate a part of our energy to growing it into something substantial. Such an "energized" thought will then stick and call us out on every opportunity to feed on the remaining energy we have.

Some of these thoughts grow so powerful that they turn into memories that weaken us for many years to come. Even though we may not even be aware of them being hidden somewhere in the labyrinth of our mind.

Such a memory is like a company employee who has been forgotten a long time ago. He comes to work every day, even though barely anyone remembers what exactly his responsibilities are. And to tell the truth, this lack of attention is quite convenient for him, as he can hide in his office while receiving a good salary at the end of each month.

To get carried away by a passing bad thought is one thing. To let a bad thought nestle down in your head forever is just another.

A boss who's in control would not stay frustrated about where his money is disappearing to. He would investigate why some particular individuals were hired in the first place and, should they be redundant, he would let them go for good.

Some of our emotions may be a response to distressing past experiences, fears, urges, desires, or instincts that are hidden from our conscious mind. Those we can control only when we learn to understand their message. Most of our other everyday emotions, though, are products of our conscious thoughts.

You don't feel a certain way because something has just happened to you. You feel that way based on how your mind has evaluated an event or a situation.

It means that, at one moment, certain thoughts pass through your head and you choose, of your own free will, to give attention to some of them. These thoughts then create a response in your body, an emotion.

When it's a stressful thought, our body responds to a perceived threat and uses its energy to possibly fight, flee, or freeze. The energy which it could have otherwise used to repair, develop, and grow itself. When it's a relaxing or a happy thought, the response of our body is to use its energy to improve functions it performs in many ways. That's why we simply feel good.

Do you remember that regular exercise makes your body more efficient in generating energy, even though in the interim it uses up some energy itself? Likewise, even good, positive thoughts need some of our energy to grow into a lasting source of vitality, power, and joy.

You can be in complete control of how you feel at any given moment (unless you suffer from some sort of clinical mental disorder). However, having said that, it's a pretty tough thing to do. Often almost impossible, as it may seem.

When someone drops an insult on you, for instance, you might be able to stay completely cool and dismiss their words in an instant. But what if he or she is someone you truly care about? Then the words hurt no matter how "positive" you try to be about it. The reaction of your body is rather correct in such case since you've just experienced a "threat" to your self-worth.

If we accumulate enough energy in our body, we should be able to contain negative thoughts, so they cannot keep kindling unpleasant emotions as a result. And the other way round, if we attempt to decode the bodily messages in the form of our emotions, we can better understand which ones of our needs, values, and beliefs make us point our focus onto a particular type of thoughts.

III. PEOPLE

People you actively interact with are divided into exactly two categories. Some of them charge you with their own positive energy, and some of them feed on yours.

Particularly when you're still at the starting point within the process of recovering your body and controlling your thoughts and emotions, it's more than advisable to steer clear of people that suck the valuable life energy from you. Such people are often hard to identify, and it can easily be your best friend as well as a family relative.

We can truly care about someone and be in good spirits when we meet them. Still, this person can, often unwillingly, end up drawing substantial amounts of energy out of our reserves.

Not always is it their fault, though. The energy loss we experience in relation to the behavior of a certain person in a certain situation can be linked to our own thoughts and to the emotions we fabricate ourselves. Then the question would be: Do I need to limit my contact with them? Get rid of them? Or do I prefer to keep them in my life on the condition of being able to control my mind better?

On the contrary, there are people who are able to create so much good energy on their own that they walk the Earth sharing it with others. We call them for advice or "take advantage" of what they have to offer. We all want to have them around and keep them close, especially when things are not going that well for us.

Most of us know at least one such person, but if we looked more closely, we would see that there are many more. They don't necessarily feel buoyant and joyful all the time themselves. They simply interact with you in a way that keeps your original energy reserves intact.

It's important to surround ourselves with people who share their extra energy or at least don't steal ours when we need it the most. Likewise, it's imperative to reduce the number of energy-sucking people in our lives. And if that cannot be done, at least limit our mutual contact to the minimum.

And then... the last step would be to look into a mirror and ask yourself: What person am I? Do I take energy from other people? Or do I have enough so I can share it with those who matter?

Impact

33. Listen and Learn

*E*ntrepreneurs are individuals who keep improving themselves in order to deliver better value to the world around them.

The major skill of an entrepreneur is the ability to listen.

The difference between hearing and listening lies in how much reaches our conscious mind, plus how much we record into our memory, from the conversations we lead. Many people are convinced that they are good listeners, and yet most of the information that is broadcasted towards them only scratches the surface.

Obviously, we must filter out what matters from what doesn't, but if we don't even tune in, the most valuable bits might slip through.

First, entrepreneurs need to listen to themselves carefully, so that they can identify the needs of their own body and their own mind. Second, they have to listen to other people in order to acknowledge their needs and problems, so that they can eventually address them with the solutions they build.

Entrepreneurs listen to learn, understand, and improve.

Active listening is not only about repeated nodding, frequent uh-huhs, or mirroring the other person's posture.

When we listen, we don't only wait for our turn to jump in, plotting our own part in our head. We don't interrupt. We don't look around.

We make eye contact. We keep our body relaxed. We switch off our internal dialogue and fully focus on the words, tone, and body language of the person who is talking.

And, most importantly, we pose good questions.

A **GOOD QUESTION** follows four criteria:

SPECIFIC – Avoid being vague at any cost. We're asked vague questions hundreds of times a day, and the human brain saves an array of ready-made answers for such occasions. Use relevant details to prove that you know what you're talking about and that you really care about receiving a detailed answer.

PERSONAL – Make your question personal, but not inquisitive or prying. When posing a question, repeat some parts of what has just been said to show respect for how the person views the situation. Notice the language they are using and accommodate your own speech to it.

URGENT – The question needs to be relevant and worth replying to at the given moment. If you ask a question which can wait or which is too trivial to even bother thinking about, don't expect the respondent to make an effort to share something of substance with you.

APPEALING – What do you think is the most attractive topic for most of us? "Me." People like to talk about themselves. Remember that they prefer to share things that matter to them, not to you. Don't try to get information out of them just because you're curious. Give them space to tell you about what occupies their mind.

Let's look at an example. Your partner comes home in the evening. Absentmindedly, you shoot your usual: "How was your day?"

See how it fits:
SPECIFIC: Hardly.
PERSONAL: Little.
URGENT: Not so much.
ATTRACTIVE: Nope.

What if you asked them something like: "What did your team say about the new sales plan you were working on last night?"

SPECIFIC: Yes. It offers enough detail.
PERSONAL: Yes. It focuses on a private issue.
URGENT: Yes. The event has happened recently and may be worth sharing.
ATTRACTIVE: Yes. You ask about a thing that is important to the person.

The best way to practice asking good questions is to be genuinely curious about other people. And if you say it's not possible to simply flip your brain to start caring about someone, you're wrong. By all means, you can make yourself feel whatever you want, if only you give it a shot.

If you sound like a robot that spits fabricated questions, or if you blatantly fake your interest, then the chances of receiving reasonable answers are low. However, if the other person senses that you genuinely care about what is happening in their inner world, they will most likely be happy to invite you in.

When we assume that a person is asking us to serve their personal interest, we usually choose to stand behind our protective walls. Even worse, when someone poses a question with their ears already shut, it only leaves us frustrated.

The skill of asking good questions will certainly make you a better friend, partner, or parent, but it will also make you a better team player, manager, leader, or mentor.

Good questions make a person believe that you give them 100% of your attention at a given moment. A good question makes a person open the gates to the world that they have built in their minds. A good question is your key to forging a

deeper human connection, because you acknowledge and respect what is going on inside.

In the age we live in, information is abundant. Yet, the more information we have, the harder it becomes to extract any meaningful data. A human being is confronted with a new fact or a piece of data almost every second, as long as they surround themselves with shiny screens. All this buzz makes the words of their fellow humans lost. Their attention span is too damaged.

It takes an effort to listen.

Listening is a skill like any other. It needs to be practiced and perfected on a daily basis.

Many people never find it attractive enough to invest any more of their time and energy into it. They don't appreciate the added value of being flooded with yet another dose of "useless" information. And then, when the moment comes, when they realize they want to know something of eminent interest, they are surprised by the walls they are challenged to mount and the poor quality of material they are able to obtain.

For every business, high-quality information and good data are essential since they help them make the right decisions at the right time. Besides, new technologies make it easier to stay ahead of the competition and satisfy our customers. But a successful entrepreneur also relies on their own mental capacity to catch, absorb, and process pieces of knowledge that help them connect with others and achieve what they are aiming at.

34. The Worth of an Idea

An idea is a thought like any other, and as such IT DOES HAVE LITTLE VALUE unless we invest a certain amount of our energy into it.

Many aspiring entrepreneurs would spend long days, months, or even years waiting for the right idea. Numerous business partnerships end up in conflict over ownership of a specific idea. In general, people hold ideas in high regard and attribute more value to them than these abstract concepts deserve.

Ideas are, indeed, an essential part of an entrepreneurial journey. They are the product of our creativity, which we need to foster and cultivate daily. However, ideas are merely step number two when developing a new personal or business project. Step number one is identifying a need or a problem your venture is going to address.

Starting a business based solely on an idea is like building a wall with no foundation.

The foundation is your ability to listen and learn about what people struggle with or which of their needs are not fully satisfied. Unfortunately, many new businesses are launched based exclusively on the belief of an entrepreneur that they are "in possession" of a brilliant idea. Only later on do they start investigating how to bring their product or service closer to their customers, how to persuade them to like it, or how to make them pay.

Instead of generating ideas, generate sustainable SOLUTIONS. Even though it's possible to make money while targeting human needs that don't necessarily end up improving lives, there lies the necessity to draw a line between a businessman/businesswoman and an entrepreneur.

The traditional division between for-profit and nonprofit companies forces us to choose between making money and doing good. Either we pursue financial gain or we strive to have a positive impact on the world around us.

The new generation of entrepreneurs, though, has started paying closer attention to the needs of not only individuals, but of society as a whole, our culture, and our environment. With governments of many countries not being able to deliver the results their people expect and demand, entrepreneurs stand in the front lines of battling the issues that plague their countries and communities.

Entrepreneurs drive change predominantly via business. Some call them "social" entrepreneurs. But much like a woman doesn't need to be called a "female" entrepreneur since she performs the same role as her male counterpart, an entrepreneur doesn't need a special label for their effort to improve people's lives.

Put simply, any entrepreneur should weigh how their endeavors affect society and the environment. At the same time, for-purpose oriented entrepreneurs need to develop sustainable business models to secure enough funds for its operations and for investment into innovation.

35. The Owner of an Idea

An entrepreneur of the 21st century looks for BUSINESS OPPORTUNITIES based on solving REAL PROBLEMS.

SUSTAINABILITY then lies at the intersection of:

PEOPLE – What do people need?

PLANET – How can I improve (or at least not harm) living conditions of all of us?

PROFIT – Will people pay me for my solution so I can sustain my business, invest into its growth, and possibly create jobs?

A business delivers a product or a service onto the market at a certain price based on a demand for such a product or service. The demand for the product or service is the quantity people will buy at a certain price. The individual demand is then not only influenced by the price, but also by the income of the customer, their habits, expectations, and their personal preferences, which stem from their personal needs.

Traditional businesses look for financial value. Traditional charities look for social value. And the line between these two has been blurring recently.

Enterprises that combine both financial and social returns are being called "social enterprises," and their business models are built with both profit and purpose in mind.

A person might start off with a good idea and potentially turn it into a profitable business. But an entrepreneur rather starts with a need they seek to address or a problem they hope to solve. Their key skill at this stage is their ability to observe and listen.

The second stage is where creativity comes into play. Here the entrepreneur generates ideas based on the needs and challenges he had identified before.

Creativity is not something one can just switch on whenever there's a need for it. It's a way of thinking that should always be nurtured in order for our mind to stay as open as possible, so that it can see ways others are not able to see and dare to go further than others would go.

At that point, we're getting closer to an idea that is actually worth something. Our main tools here are our analytical and communication skills. Taking into account all the alternatives we have creatively come up with, we shortlist those that follow the common SMART criteria.

Our idea/solution should then be:

Specific → What makes it the right product or service? How exactly is it going to fulfill a specific need or solve a specific problem? What are the individual benefits?

Measurable → How are we going to know that we have succeeded? What are the criteria to track our progress?

Attainable	➡ Is it realistic? Can we get hold of relevant technology or knowledge? Do we have a sufficient budget?
Relevant	➡ Is the idea applicable to the situation I am trying to address? Is the market big enough? Is the need or the problem worth anyone's attention?
Time-specific	➡ What is the roadmap and its individual deadlines? Is it feasible within the next 2, 5, 10... years?

While following these steps, we move from the world of imagination to the world of logic. While at stage two (idea generation), we gave our thoughts the freedom to diverge in all directions, at stage three (idea validation), we bring them back in to assess their strengths and weaknesses.

An important part of the idea validation stage is going back to our listening skills since we need to keep communicating with our target users. Is this the solution they would consider satisfying? Would they pay for it?

The feedback we gather helps us build a solution that is not solely derived from our "idea" but is in touch with genuine needs of our customers. In fact, we should not "fall in love" with our ideas too deeply, otherwise they would prevent us from staying flexible, modifying what needs to be modified, or even changing our product or service from scratch based on what we hear when we truly listen.

The last stage is when we deliver and execute with the help of our problem-solving skills. In fact, the definition of an entrepreneur could be shortened to "a problem-solver."

Ideas are free. Any of us is capable of coming up with a myriad of ideas if we only dip deep enough into our knowledge and creativity. However, few of us are willing to invest a considerable chunk of our energy, our time, and our money into bringing an idea to life.

Entrepreneurship is not a domain of fast returns. There are a few companies that grow damn fast, so their founders and investors can cash in quickly. But plenty of problems that require solving call for an entrepreneur who is patient and tenacious.

Often, such entrepreneurs live on a limited personal income, or give it up altogether, for a considerable time. They spend months, or even long years, building something without a single guarantee of any kind of reward.

How is it possible for them to persevere? What makes a person get up and keep walking after they had fallen to their knees over and over?

If they were in business for an idea, they would give up fast. They would build it and attempt at selling it. If it didn't work, they would readily move onto something better.

Failing fast is a mantra of many individuals who aspire to build successful companies. If their product is not able to make money, at least they learn about it without delay, without investing any extra resources.

Nevertheless, entrepreneurs who seek value in whatever they are working on don't give up as easily. As long as they believe that it improves lives of the people they target, they do their best to make their solution work.

It may take a lot of experimenting and a lot of temporary failures to create something that meets the needs and expectations of people who are often not aware of those themselves. That's why entrepreneurs are not driven solely by the vision of profit, but by the vision of purpose as well.

The world needs entrepreneurs. It needs people who constantly look for ways to make other people's lives easier. It needs people who don't sit idly in the corner waiting for things to improve themselves, or for governments to do their job.

36. Touch a Human Life

*I*t was Oscar Wilde who had one of his characters say, *"A cynic is a man who knows the price of everything, and the value of nothing."* The statement then earns a snap response from the character's fellow: *"And a sentimentalist is a man who sees an absurd value in everything and doesn't know the market price of any single thing."*

If that is so, where is the truth? What are the criteria of succeeding if one needs to choose between the capitalist penchant for profit or the value-driven idealist sentiment? And if one does make their choice, wouldn't they be judged regardless of which way they go?

As such, some entrepreneurs seem to be building castles in the air. They tend to chase righteous ideals or see value in things that others deem worthless. Often they pursue innovative or charitable goals out of conviction rather than calculation.

On the contrary, certain individuals call themselves entrepreneurs, although their one and only criteria of success is how much money they can make out of their hard work or talent. These people are often extremely competent and good at doing business in the sense of generating profit, creating jobs, and beating the competition. Not always, though, do they keep in mind how many human lives, and to what extent, they have touched along the way.

Touch one human life and you will change the whole world.

Arguably, there's nothing wrong with either ideals or money in principle, once we realize that both can indeed be kept in solid balance. A person may call themselves an entrepreneur if they are dedicated to continuous self-improvement that allows them to deliver long-lasting positive value to both themselves and to the people they serve with their skills, knowledge, time, and energy.

You cannot help others unless you help yourself first.

However, as long as they aspire to sustain themselves and their team, foster innovation, and grow in order to improve the lives of as many people as possible, they cannot afford to ignore the necessity of developing a justifiable business model.

Different entrepreneurs may have their benchmarks of success set at different levels. Some of them won't ever make an extra dime of what they have achieved for themselves, yet they sleep in peace since they know that at every single moment, they have been doing their best to learn and to make something that brings value to other people.

In contrast, some will build companies worth millions of dollars. And they will either keep learning, innovating, and fixing their eye on delivering a valuable product or service, or the entrepreneur in them will give way to the businessman or businesswoman who ties all their decisions to financial and economic criteria.

Is such a person—one who puts the financial and economic value above the social, cultural, ethical, moral, or environmental one—a cynic?

Maybe, yes. Or, maybe, they simply follow their own personal interest, which is an integral nature of all human beings. Maybe their endeavors benefit our societies and economies in ways not everyone is able to see at first.

What makes a person who calls themselves an entrepreneur different is their QUEST FOR POSITIVE IMPACT in every bit of their efforts.

All the time, energy, and money of an entrepreneur who has invested them in personal growth and in bringing value to others are never lost. It's not only about an investment into a better future, it's about making the present worth living. The stronger we become, the more choices we create for ourselves. The more we learn, the more we expand the garden of our mind, which in return will assist us in experiencing joy and happiness.

It's a cruel irony that most people choose to live their lives being unhappy. They spend their days wading through

ENVY
ENVY
FEAR
ANGER
DISGUST
DISGUST
FEAR
ANGER
SADNESS
SADNESS
DISGUST

stress, despair, anger, frustration. They do dream of the day when the state of mind called "happiness" will knock on their doors and change everything from top to bottom, yet, simultaneously, they don't accept responsibility for their own thoughts and feelings. Day by day, they pick harmless fragments that pass through their heads and grow them into insatiable monsters that nest in their souls in order to eventually suck in all the light.

Every moment we spend sunken in worries, fear, or tears is a moment wasted. Still, we invest a huge amount of our energy into everything else but being happy. We believe happiness is something that depends entirely on external factors. How people treat us, how much they like us, or what they think about us. How much we can buy or where we live. If we have a job that sucks or if we have a prestigious degree and an enviable career. If we date or are married to the right person or if our sex life is as good or better as that of other people.

It's as if we were playing a video game, trying to collect happiness points by doing the right thing, moving in the right direction or making the right decision. And since we're never sure what the next level is going to look like, we constantly feel as if we're failing. Or that others are failing us for that matter.

People who have very little often smile, or even laugh, much more than people who have had the privilege of always having something to eat and being able to sleep in a bed under a safe roof. When you look around big cities, the places with the highest concentrations of wealth, people on the streets rarely smile. They look stressed, restless;

they walk fast. People who don't have "enough" invite the concept of failure to spoil their blood. People who have a lot seek professional therapy to figure out what is wrong with them, or what prevents them from experiencing peace and joy.

A physically, mentally, and spiritually strong person can choose to feel whatever they want to, at any given moment. That's why it is so important to never cease improving ourselves because then we always have a choice, we have control of how our life is going to be. And a person who chooses their vocation to be an entrepreneur uses the gift of their humanity to create things that benefit their fellow men and women.

The risk factor of doing business is considerably high. No one wants to wake up one day and realize that their savings are gone for nothing, or that they have spent years working on something that didn't bring any tangible result. That's why it's so important to not only listen to others but to oneself in the first place. We need to remember and review our beliefs regarding what we do and why we do it.

Here and there, we should ask ourselves some (uncomfortable) questions:

Are my mind and body strong?

Do I keep learning and improving myself?

Is there a value in what I'm doing?

Every moment
we spend sunken
in worries, fear, or tears
is a moment wasted.

If the answer is no, then there's no way to move anywhere before we "fix" ourselves. If the answer is yes, we shall follow up with these:

Am I doing my best to offer the best possible result?

Is my business sustainable, both in terms of money and society, as well as the environment?

The answers to the first three questions should be "yes" no matter at what stage of our career we find ourselves. Even if we're trapped in a job we hate, if our business is losing money, or if we're unemployed, we need to keep our mind clear and sharp and our body fit and healthy. Only then do we have enough energy to use for:
a) Learning
b) Creativity
c) Building

Many people do it just the other way around. When they feel stuck in a place in their life they don't want to be, they try very hard to figure out in which direction to move next. They ask themselves:

"What should I do with my life?"
rather than
"How can I make myself stronger and more valuable to others?"

Especially the idea of making oneself valuable to other people can be hard to digest for many as they often believe it is "the other people" in the first place who make their life difficult.

However, first, there will never be any money in your pocket, unless you bring value to other people. Second, the value you can offer heavily depends on how much you know and how much you can do, so if there's something wrong with your job or business situation, boosting your personal growth is the obvious way to go.

Usually, we are unable to move forward, because we lack energy, mental clarity, and inner drive to do so. If we keep our bodies strong and our mind open and creative, if we improve ourselves even the tiniest bit every day, and if we strive to offer some value to the people around us, the right opportunities will present themselves easily and as if "by magic."

The questions mentioned above are perhaps not common for the majority of people in business. They would rather ask themselves: How can I increase my profit? What do I need to do to scale fast? Where do I find the best people for my team? How do I become a better leader? What is my competition doing?

Such questions are undoubtedly significant, yet they are merely operational—the answers to them change over time depending on the current stage of our business.

The purpose of a life spent in the skin of an entrepreneur lies at the intersection of:

LEARNING – You're great at what you do.

VALUE – People need what you do.

PASSION – You find joy in what you do.

PROFESSION – You are rewarded for what you do.

It boils right down to that. Entrepreneurship doesn't just talk about passion for our various projects. Entrepreneurship doesn't exist merely to proliferate profitable companies. Entrepreneurship doesn't serve the sole purpose of giving people what they want. Entrepreneurship is not only a choice of lifestyle.

ENTREPRENEURSHIP IS ABOUT MAKING A POSITIVE **IMPACT** WHILE HAVING FULL **CONTROL** OF OUR EXPERIENCE AND LIVING OUR LIFE WITH A **PURPOSE**.

37. Why Should You Care?

Why should we even care about what is happening around us? Mind that we participate in various elections to choose our leaders and our governments. They'd better do their job and make our lives better! Then we can finally live in peace and focus on what is important to us: our work, our family, our own happiness. Right?

But is this the reality? When there is a problem in our neighborhood, our community, our country… is there also always someone who jumps right in to build an efficient and sustainable solution? And if so, are those people the ones we have selected to represent our best interests?

Rarely.

Every government and every official political representation follows their very own immediate interests. Quite naturally. If we are lucky, some of those interests contain policies that aim at improving the lives of their citizens. However, not always do they work, nor do they always meet all our demands and needs.

If we are less lucky, those interests may result in economic downturns, nasty wars, public unrest, or interracial hatred. Who to call then?

ENTREPRENEURS COULD BE THE HEROES OF THE MODERN AGE. Not because they sacrifice their interests for the greater good. An entrepreneur is not an ascetic altruist who places the needs of other people above their own. Their spirit is free by nature, and when they see a problem they may be able to solve with their skills and resources, they don't wait for some other individual or entity to get the job done instead.

Thanks to the new technologies, we're more connected to the outer world than ever. We can talk to friends or teammates who live thousands of kilometers away from us. The information about what is happening anywhere on Earth reaches us often within mere seconds. More than ever before, we are an active part of the global community, regardless of our place of birth.

It's questionable, though, if we enjoy the fruits of technology or rather allow it to ruin our lives.

Yes, we can talk to anyone anywhere in the world, but in reality, we have stopped talking and listening to each other. We exchange texts and images, and when we do talk, we're unable to focus on the words of the other person, since our electronic devices have made us addicted to a constant stream of alternative entertainment.

On the other hand, technology provides easy and affordable tools for entrepreneurs to connect with various audiences and customers all around the world. More than ever, an individual can affect a massive number of people even with limited financial resources.

When we take part in the worldwide exchange of ideas, knowledge, and most importantly, innovation, we are presented with an opportunity to contribute to a better life quality of a multitude of individuals. Such exchange then flows both ways. Helping people improve their lives simultaneously leads to improving our own.

Due to the global interconnectivity, we are directly affected by what is happening not only within but also far from our borders. When we deliver value outside of our private and community circles, for the good of all the people in our country, the positive boomerang effect will eventually reach us and those we care about. Likewise, when we deliver value beyond the frontiers of our nation or state, we may support the political stability and economic prosperity in other territories. Our activities can foster dialogue, collaboration, and further advancement of beneficial innovation.

38. Proactive and Reactive Impact

The impact you have on others can be either:

PROACTIVE ➡ You create new or better value for yourself and other people.

REACTIVE ➡ You take ownership of the issues that affect...

You

Your activities make an impact on your body, your soul, and your spirit.

Your Inner Circle

Your activities impact the people you care about most (your life partner, family, close friends...). These individuals contribute significantly to who you are and ignoring them based on the premise of "business first" is as if you threw your crew overboard because you believed that with less weight your ship would get to the final destination much faster.

Your Community Circle

Your activities have an impact on the communities you're an active and integral part of. These are usually linked to the place you live (your neighborhood, village, city, your country...), your work (your team, your company, your partners...), your interests (clubs, associations, internet groups...), or your personal growth (school, university...). When you create some positive value for them, you gain much more in return. They grow, you grow. They prosper, you prosper.

The Outer Circle

The aforementioned global interconnectivity originates not only from an enhanced communication and exchange of information, but also from technologies that allow faster travel of people, delivery of goods, and flow of money. Globalization makes individuals, companies, and nations dependent on each other more than they had been at any time in history. State of the economy of one country can fundamentally influence many others. A product we build for one market can spread and impact many other markets.

Global trade is a privilege of multinational corporations no more. A single entrepreneur can take advantage of the Internet and digital technologies to sell products and services in various foreign countries. People collaborate and share ideas without ever meeting each other. Cultural values cross borders and transform how we think, behave, and communicate with each other. The globalized human interactions make economic and cultural differences come under the spotlight, causing potential conflict between both individuals and nations.

All in all, it's practically impossible to separate what we do as entrepreneurs from the rest of the world.

Creating new jobs and cultivating entrepreneurship

When you give people work, you directly impact and enrich their lives. Work is a basic human need that is closely tied to the concepts of dignity, fulfillment, security, and self-sufficiency. Unemployment, on the contrary, not only harms the overall economy of a country, but also the mental and physical health of individuals, the family and social stability, or usage and distribution of skills.

Delivering a valuable product or service

When you develop a product or a service that meets human needs or addresses people's problems, you can have a considerable positive impact. The larger the market for what you do, the larger the number of people whose lives you can improve, and the bigger the chances of your business being profitable.

Facilitating access to information and knowledge

When you contribute to the flow of information, knowledge sharing, innovation, and exchange of ideas, you impact the whole world. Yes, too much information may and often does have a negative impact on our learning, communication, and decision-making skills, or our productivity. On the other hand, better access to information and education typically results in a much wider variety of personal and professional choices.

Improving the living environment

The importance of protecting our Mother Nature is a no-brainer. Sustainable entrepreneurship is the future if we don't wish to end up on an uninhabitable planet. The air we breathe, the food we eat, the water we drink, the space we occupy, the fauna and flora that surround us, the resources we use and share... all these need to be taken into account when assessing the outcome of our business activities.

Improving the living conditions of disadvantaged people

Some groups of people need our help more than others. Even though, in theory, it's the job of our governments to make sure that all the citizens have equal rights and opportunities, the reality tends to be quite different. Entrepreneurs are those who could step in and play a part in forming a more democratic and equal society.

Preserving tradition and culture

Common beliefs, customs, and values strengthen the connections between individuals and communities. As entrepreneurs, we should do our best to understand and appreciate them. The more we identify with people of similar backgrounds and mindsets, the more likely we are to be willing to take ownership of their issues.

Encouraging human communication and dialogue

The proliferation of new technologies in the recent decades has made it rather difficult for us to balance the

TAKE CARE
OF THE
WORLD...
...AND THE WORLD
WILL TAKE CARE
OF YOU.

good and the bad of various means of communication. The world is connected more than we can imagine and information can instantly get spread out to all four corners of the world. We need to make sure that continuous and constructive dialogue is ensured, so that we understand each other's viewpoints and jointly find solutions to both our shared and unique issues.

TAKE CARE OF THE WORLD AND THE WORLD WILL TAKE CARE OF YOU.

What now?

39. Dreaming Small?

A dream is a photograph on which you see your-self in a world that is more beautiful than the one you currently live in. Often we have whole long walls of our homes covered with such photographs, and we get caught up in their tales. There are days when we venture out and make an effort to find the places from those images. Sometimes, we decide not to leave the house at all and enjoy the comfort of what we already know and what has so far worked for us rather well.

DREAMS CHANGE BUT A PURPOSE LASTS.

You have heard people tell you that you should "follow your dreams." Maybe you agreed with them at first, but later were left confused.

"Which one of my dreams? I have so many!"

Or else: "I don't dream about anything in particular, even though they tell me I should. But isn't it just silly, chasing a fantasy instead of hustling to survive in this messy world?"

People also say, "Dream big!" What they really mean is that you should SET YOURSELF AMBITIOUS GOALS AND WORK HARD ON ACHIEVING THEM.

Challenging goals play a powerful role in our lives. Even if we never reached them, they push us to try harder. Thanks to them, we are, at all times, on the lookout for new opportunities to improve and grow. As Niccollò Machiavelli wrote:

"A wise man ought always to follow the paths beaten by great men, and to imitate those who have been supreme, so that if his ability does not equal theirs, at least it will savour of it. Let him act like the clever archers who, designing to hit the mark which yet appears too far distant, and knowing the limits to which the strength of their bow attains, take aim much higher than the mark, not to reach by their strength or arrow to so great a height, but to be able with the aid of so high an aim to hit the mark they wish to reach."

In simple terms, AIMING HIGHER HELPS YOU REACH THE POINT YOU ACTUALLY WANT TO HIT.

The road towards your goals can lead you to brand new ones you had no idea about when you set off. That's why you need not worry right now if the goals you've chosen for yourself are the "perfect" ones, the "right" ones. If they're something you really, really want right now, then do your best to get there. Regardless of what happens next, you will become a stronger, better person along the way, and that's what matters.

To change a route, if needed, is not a bad thing. New priorities may arise at any point, and embracing them doesn't make you a weakling or a drifter, as long as you've been GIVING YOUR MAXIMUM to arrive at your original destination.

For some people, though, it's frustrating to have only little or no idea what this final destination should look like. They believe there is only one right answer to how their lives should reel off from their childhood until their death. The inability to find the "true meaning" to their existence crushes them heavily, even if only subconsciously.

Human beings tend to assume that a big part of their existence is out of their control. They are convinced that their choices have only limited impact on what happens to them.

Wrong partner. Business failure. Illness. Debt. Anxiety. Boring job. Insufficient education. Family trauma. Broken marriage. Overweight. Insomnia. Procrastination. Professional burnout. Overwork. Harassment. Loneliness. Unreliable friends. Addiction. Fear. Humiliation. Shame... and so on, and so on.

What can I do?! Maybe it was meant to be. However hard I try, I can't escape from the cage I've been imprisoned in since I was born.

Yes, even though you might be trying hard, working hard, and doing your best on most of your days, there will always be obstacles to face. Rarely can you change external circumstances, but you can indeed have control of how they affect your thinking, your choices, and your health. Just as your personal and professional goals are mere milestones on your overall journey, the challenges that seem to make your life difficult are mere drawbacks that test your endurance and will to keep going.

You can do a lot to reduce the risk of falling ill by treating your body well. You can heal your soul so you don't attract the wrong people. You can avoid stress as a default response to the behavior of others.

You have control, yet too often you choose to give in. Or you wait for something or someone who will, as if by a miracle, solve everything for you.

People would ask themselves, "Why? Why is this happening to me? Why do I need to suffer so much? Is this the purpose?"

The purpose of your life is not something that some other entity has decided for you. It is not something you either follow or you fail. You create and shape the purpose yourself. Look for it by following the signals of your heart, which lets you know whenever it feels that you are where you should be, doing what you want to be doing.

In this spirit, the small dreams are as important as the big, lofty ones. Small dreams are easier to envisage. They bring joy to our souls at the very instant we picture them in our heads.

Perhaps you prefer to lock them up in the world of your imagination since they seem too self-indulgent to pursue. As much as you find pleasure in meeting your desires and fulfilling those humble fantasies now and then, you consider them to be detours that stall your progress on the way to a real success.

Nothing can be further from the truth.

Small dreams are indispensable to your wellbeing and prosperity. They help you explore yourself and learn who you are. Each and every time you experience inner peace, gratitude, and joy, magic happens. You create memories that are a priceless source of positive energy for the rest of your life. You awaken your spirit to guide you on your next steps. Your body heals, and the garden of your mind flourishes.

Making your small dreams come true will eventually help you reveal your purpose. YOU NEED TO HONOR YOUR RIGHT TO BE HAPPY. You need to assume responsibility for experiencing fulfillment.

THE MEANING OF YOUR LIFE IS TO DO ALL YOU CAN TO FREE YOURSELF FROM YOUR CAGE AND FLY.

40. Ten Commandments

There is no perfect moment for you to start calling yourself who you feel you really are. There are no objective criteria imposed on you from above to evaluate and judge your choices. The only thing you need to do is to celebrate the gift of life by giving the best of yourself, seeking joy, and creating something of value.

> You are who you choose to be. No one can tell you otherwise.

Anyone can become an entrepreneur at any point in their lives, regardless of their background, gender, age, past career choices, financial situation, or level of experience. Entrepreneurship is not about individual achievements and resources one has at their disposal. It's a mindset of brave human individuals who have understood that their time on Earth is absolutely limited and who don't wait for someone else to make their existence worthy and pleasurable.

When they see a problem they could solve, they give it a try. When they face an obstacle, they fight it.

Entrepreneurs are not superheroes to worship or envy. But it's good to have them around since they always do all that is in their power to move the world a bit forward.

1. Don't wait for the perfect day

You will never have just the right amount of experience and just the right amount of resources to set things in motion. If you want to do it, start now. There is no project too small. There is no task too difficult. Things may not always work out as planned, but keep in mind that every step counts towards you being a strong and competent individual.

2. Heal your body

You have five fingers on your hand. Use them to remember that you can be in control of your body if you pay attention to:

Breathing

Sleeping

Drinking

Eating

Moving

3. Control your thoughts

Many of the thoughts that pass through your head are but random fragments of neutral charge. It means they are neither positive nor negative unless you pay attention to them, judge them, and grow them into a message that appears real.

If you gain control of what enters and resides in your mind, your whole life will transform, starting with your mental and physical health, your self-worth, relationships, and opportunities you will attract.

4. Preserve your energy

Your first job as an entrepreneur is to take care of yourself. The more energy you have, the closer you are to success.

Get rid of everything that makes it go away, such as individuals who feed on your vitality or thoughts that result in unpleasant emotions. Build up your own energy reserves by surrounding yourself with positive people, maintain a good health of your body and mind, and seek moments of joy.

5. Always improve yourself

You need to keep improving yourself. Not because you aren't perfect. You are enough, and you are worthy just as you are. However, when you make your body and mind stronger, you can preserve and generate sufficient energy to achieve anything you want. Besides, when you learn, broaden your mind, and develop new skills, you continuously expand the world of opportunities that is laid out in front of you.

6. Learn to listen

You can't learn to listen to others if you don't learn to listen to your own needs. Your body talks to you every day, so don't ignore it. Your mind needs your help as well, in order to stay clear, creative, and focused, so just give it a hand.

When you talk to others, be genuinely curious. Ask good questions and collect material that will help you build something of value one day.

7. Look around

Listening is one thing, observing is another. Many people look but they don't really see.

We tend to ignore the absolute majority of inspiration, beauty, noises, smells, hints... that surround us. Great entrepreneurs are good observers. Since they perpetually nurture their creativity, they are capable of coming up with solutions others deem unsolvable.

8. Create value

The essence of your mission as an entrepreneur is to deliver value not only to yourself but to other people whose needs you appreciate.

As an aspiring entrepreneur, keep learning. Once you decide to build and deliver sustainable value, you become an entrepreneur. If you find joy in what you do, you're a happy entrepreneur. And if your solution makes money, you're a profitable entrepreneur.

9. Respect your time

Your time is the most valuable resource you have, so treat it as such.

Make it a priority to develop good habits and ditch the bad ones.

Never forget that time to relax is as important as time to work because that is when you refill your energy reserves, grow, and cultivate creativity.

Look for the moments that make your heart vibrate with joy. They will make you a better person and they will help you find your purpose in life and work.

About the Author

Kristyna Zapletal is an advocate of entrepreneurship with positive social and environmental impact. As a coach, she helps inspiring individuals realize their most daring visions. As an educator, she has traveled the world teaching entrepreneurs how to build their digital skills. Follow her writing at mindfulentrepreneurship.com.